Truth Missiles

The Explosive Parables of Jesus

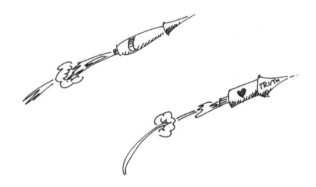

Peter JR Smith

ISBN 978-1-0684400-0-7 (paperback)

ISBN 978-1-0684400-1-4 (eBook)

 Published by The Talking Donkey - talkingdonkey.blog

Dedication

To my wife, Francine, and our children, who have been (mostly) patient all the hours I've sat writing...

To our church, and everyone who has encouraged me by reading my drafts...

... my thanks, and my love.

Contents

About This Book

During the national Covid lockdown, our rector, Steve Wookey, asked if I'd write a short set of "thoughts" for St. David's Church. I chose the parables of Mark, because I had been reading them at the time. I set about writing a few short talks but while I was doing so I began to ask myself: when did I last do any real thinking on these little stories? I honestly couldn't think of a time, not since childhood. Later, after the talks were delivered, a number of people got in touch saying the same thing; they couldn't remember the last time they'd stopped to think about the parables. It turned out I wasn't the only person who'd learned them at Sunday school but never returned to them again...

But these are the actual stories Jesus told two thousand years ago to ordinary (adult) people like you and me. They are the *explosive* stories that changed the world forever. They really are the little stories with a big impact! They are the most direct teachings of Jesus, a "fragment of the original rock of tradition".[1] So, if Jesus is our teacher, we should be familiar with them, and clear about what they mean!

So this convinced me to spend a lot more time in the parables. This book is a result of that time, and an attempt to form it into something useful - for you.

While assembling the book I had to decide how to order or categorise them. I chose to arrange them (roughly) in the order they

---

[1] Joachim Jeremias – in his introduction to *The Parables of Jesus*.

are given to us in the Gospels.[2] This way you can see how the focus of Jesus' teaching shifts while events unfolded over the course of his ministry. I hope you enjoy that.

In some places I have included short stories of my own that I've called "Not-a-Parables" (to remind you they are *not* Jesus' parables!). These tackle the same themes, borrowing themes from the original stories and dropping them into a modern setting. I wanted to reproduce how ordinary, yet surprising, the original stories would have sounded to Jesus' first audience. I'm not the first person to attempt this but I hope mine are thought-provoking. Of course, because these are not Jesus' stories, if you find them distracting, or confusing, please skip over them. You'll probably like some more than others!

I expect most people reading this book would call themselves a Christian, but you might simply have an interest in the things Jesus taught, and hope to learn a bit more about the parables. In either case, I pray you find something useful here.

God bless,

Peter

---

[2] Other ordering systems *are* available! You could group them topically or by audience, for instance... But I have chosen to do so chronologically, some of which is arguable because the parables don't always appear in the same order across the Gospels – either because the Gospel writers assembled their material non-chronologically or because Jesus repeated his parables or used similar parables in different circumstances.

Introduction

Our churches are full of people talking about how much we love Jesus. This is good! But Jesus said, "If you love me, you will keep my commandments." (John 14:15) Sadly, however heartfelt, we don't always manage to turn love into obedience, because, while we take great comfort in being loved, we don't like being told what to do. So we become disciples with selective hearing – we hear the comforting things about love very loudly but we're much less ready to hear those commandments. Parents will have noticed the same pattern with their children; picture this realistic scene:

- *Daddy?*
- *Yes, son?*
- *I love you, Dad.*
- *Thank you, son. I love you too. Did you tidy your room up like I asked?*
- *I made you this card. It's got a big heart on the front because I love you, and a dinosaur in a car. I was going to tidy my room but I started thinking about how much I love you and how much you like dinosaurs and cars, so, no, I haven't tidied my room. I used all my new colours.*
- *It does have a lot of colours. Will you tidy your room now?*
- *Maybe. Daddy?*
- *Yes, son?*
- *I'm hungry now; can we eat?*

In a perfect world, love and obedience would be entwined, so if Jesus is who we love, he should also be who we obey. So it follows: to love and obey, we need as much clarity as possible about what he wants to teach us.

Jesus delivered a lot of his teaching through parables. This wasn't unique to Jesus, but Jesus was *the master* of them, and the way he used them was explosive. By the grace of God, Jesus' parables are recorded for us in the Bible, so Christians who love him can hear his teaching today, in the same form, and with the same clarity as his first audience.

What Is a Parable?

G ood question. But let's start with three things they're not. Firstly, they're not *children's stories*. Yes, they can be good to teach in Sunday school, and yes, children can learn from them. But we shouldn't think of them as Jesus' youth ministry, or expect to grow out of them and move onto the complicated things Paul wrote. You want to know how to follow Christ? Well, in the parables you have the direct teachings of Christ; what more could you ask for?!

Secondly, they're not *comfortable reading*. Jesus' stories were so unsettling to the most powerful people of his time that he was arrested and executed.

Finally, a parable is not a *simple way of explaining something complicated*. If we're careful listeners, the truth in the parables is usually quite simple in the first place. More often than not, the tricky bit is that we don't want to hear it!

A parable is like a painting with words, a way of explaining something using an illustrative form of speech.[3] Anything from a

---

[3] Such as a simile, a metaphor, an allegory, or an example story…

simple one-liner to a long story could be called a parable.[4] Interestingly (for people who get excited about this sort of thing), the word "parable" came from *para-* "beside" *-bole* "a throw". So the way a parable works is by throwing a new idea *alongside* the subject. The listener has to want to understand, and do some of the work themselves, but this effort means the truth will be unlocked, or exploded, from *inside* the mind of the listener.

The human heart is stubborn, and about as thick-skinned as an armour-plated military bunker buried deep underground. Human nature is to want to stay selfish and live for ourselves. So if an uncomfortable truth is heading for our hearts, we treat it like an

attack, and hide in our defences. But, for "those with ears to hear", the parables engage our minds and deliver the truth directly to *inside* our hearts.

In that sense we can think of a parable as a "truth missile", a way of teaching that has two parts. One part is the story, a delivery system that cuts right through the bunker wall. The other part is the truth we need to learn, embedded in the story itself. The dot-connecting, which happens after we hear the story, is how we receive the truth.

---

[4] Actually, this makes it hard to agree how many parables are in the Bible, because it depends where you draw the line.

A great example of this, from before the birth of Jesus, is found in the Bible, at 2 Samuel 12, where Nathan confronts King David about his affair with Bathsheba and plotting the death of her husband, Uriah, to cover it up. Nathan uses a parable to deliver God's message, and it landed right in David's heart. As a result he was humbled and looked to God for forgiveness.

Jesus said he spoke in parables so that only those "with ears to hear, may hear". To some the secrets are given, to others they are concealed. (Matthew 13:10–17) If you are ready to hear the truth, you receive it readily from these explosive stories. But what about those *without* ears to hear? Anyone intent on rejecting Jesus finds that the truth is obscured by the parables – the parables just muddy the waters. Even what understanding they had is taken away from them.

In this way, mysteriously, Jesus uses the parables to divide those who will hear and those who won't. Nobody is allowed to sit on the fence. He pushes us off it, one side or the other.

A Great Teacher... or Lord?

L ots of people take the view that Jesus was simply a great human teacher, nothing more. But how many of them, we wonder, actually read his teaching before reaching that conclusion? When Douglas Adams summed up Jesus' ministry at the opening of *The Hitchhiker's Guide to the Galaxy* he did it like this:

"2,000 years ago one man got nailed to a tree for saying how great it would be if everyone was nice to each other for a change."

Being nice to each other is a common view of what it means to be Christian. Turning Christ-ianity into "trying-not-to-upset-anyone-ity". But Jesus said a lot of things that upset people an awful lot, so this cannot be right. Jesus didn't get nailed to a tree for saying it's great to be nice.[5]

Jesus was not on a mission to be nice. Instead he laid out facts about the Kingdom of God, and the Son of Man, *who he was* and what we should do about it. He left us to choose what we believe about him: either he's insane or he's the promised son of God. There's no middle ground, the only options are the extreme ones, to either worship him or kill him. CS Lewis said it well:

I am trying here to prevent anyone saying the foolish thing that people often say about Him: I'm ready to accept Jesus to be a great moral teacher, but I don't accept his claim to be God. That is the one thing we must not say. A man who was merely a man and said the kind of things Jesus said would not be a great moral teacher. He would either be a lunatic, on the level with the man who says he's a poached egg, or else he would be the devil of Hell. You must make your choice. Either this man was, and is the Son of God, or else a madman or something worse. You can shut him up as a fool, you can spit at him as a daemon or you can fall at his feet and call him Lord and God, but let us not come up with any patronising nonsense about his being a great human teacher. He has not left that open to us. He did not intend to.

---

[5] This is good news for nice people everywhere, Christian or otherwise.

The Great Challenge of the Parables

I'm hoping that by collecting these parables together the main thrust of Jesus' teaching is clear.

I'm hoping that what comes through loudest is the most important challenge of the parables, the challenge of how to respond personally to Jesus. Accept or Reject. Worship or Kill. Like CS Lewis said, that was his intention. There is no sitting on the fence. If Jesus wasn't the son of God, then he was a dangerous, fig tree-killing, temple market-destroying maniac. Take your pick carefully. Some people will examine his teaching and reject Jesus. I can't agree with them but it's far more consistent than calling him a "great teacher" or a "nice guy".

I'm hoping, however, that your conclusion is this: Jesus is the son of God, and his teaching is the true wisdom, the word of God, revealed to us all. And I'm hoping and praying this collection of parables is an encouragement to you in your faith.

Let's begin.

Prologue – about 980 BC[6]

N athan! Join me."

He was pleased to see a friendly face; perhaps this would be a welcome distraction. Nathan was a trusted messenger from the Lord, and David had come to take everything from the lips of Nathan as though it were directly spoken from God. This side of the grave, the company of a prophet like Nathan would be as close to God as most of us will ever get. He dismissed the others. Nathan looked sombre.

"I have a message."

"Please begin."

"There were two men in the same city; one was rich, the other poor. The rich man had huge flocks of sheep, herds of cattle. The poor man had nothing but one little female lamb, which he had bought and raised. It grew up with him and his children as a member of the family. It ate off his plate and drank from his cup and slept on his bed. It was like a daughter to him."

David smiled. Nathan continued, "One day a traveller dropped in on the rich man. He was too stingy to take an animal from his own herds or flocks to make a meal for his visitor, so he took the poor man's lamb and prepared a meal to set before his guest."

---

[6] Read 2 Samuel 12.

David leaped out of his seat. "Who is this man? He deserves to be torn apart. He'll be made to pay it back, four times over! The stingy criminal!" Nathan stood silent; the king was waiting for an answer – doing his best to read Nathan's expression. What was the rest of the story? Was this rich man real or a vision? Perhaps one of his subjects? Did he know him? A member of his court?

David knew God's law and stood ready to defend it. Surely this rich man would suffer. Those who God has blessed so richly must never forget it. To grasp what has been entrusted them, and trample the needy to hold onto your excess? This was shameful. He treated the words of God with contempt. "Well?" David insisted, narrowing his eyes...

"You are the man." said Nathan.

Part 1

The New Kingdom Dawns

Jesus' Earliest Parables

Jesus begins his ministry with a call to respond, then teaches what the Kingdom of God is like and how its citizens need to act...

1 What Are You Building Your Life On?

The Two Builders

Matthew 7:24-27

Everyone then who hears these words of mine and does them will be like a wise man who built his house on the rock. And the rain fell, and the floods came, and the winds blew and beat on that house, but it did not fall, because it had been founded on the rock. And everyone who hears these words of mine and does not do them will be like a foolish man who built his house on the sand. And the rain fell, and the floods came, and the winds blew and beat on that house, and it fell, and great was the fall of it.

It's a summer day in our garden in rural Warwickshire. My grandfather – a large man in tight shorts – is slowly lowering himself into a deck chair. We hear a sound, like a long zipping noise and the splitting of wood. When we look up, Grandad is on the grass, tangled in chair wreckage and trying to save his lemonade. That was the day our grandad became a living parable, and the lesson he taught us was this: before you put your weight on something, you need to be confident it's strong enough to hold you.

Imagine you were part of the crowd that turned up to hear Jesus teaching at the Sermon on the Mount.[7] Jesus had spoken about divorce, anger, charity, lust, hatred, prayer and anxiety. He had broadcast God's wisdom to the crowd. But then he finished the day with a little story about two men building their homes. Perhaps some of the crowd wondered why. Well, let's take a look.

In the parable, one man begins by finding rock. The local ground would have had a shallow depth of sandy topsoil with solid stone beneath. So this *wise* builder started by digging down, removing the sand, until he found something solid to build on. This is why he's called *wise*. The other builder made a phenomenally poor decision. He got his tools out and built his walls directly on the sand. This is why he's called *a fool*.

Once the two homes were built, everything was going fine for both homebuilders, until the weather turned. Now the storms and rain came along and the floodwater rose. The wind blew against both houses. It blew hard; life is like that sometimes. Whether you live in a wise house or a foolish house, you still get the same storms.

In both cases the sand was washed away, but here's the difference: only the fool had built his house on it. So, for him, when the sand moved, there was nothing left to hold up his walls, so his house came down.

"... and great was the fall of it!"

---

[7] Sermon on the Mount, Matthew 5–7; The Two Builders is also found in the Sermon on the Plain, Luke 6.

So why was Jesus talking about building? The crowd didn't need construction lessons; they knew how to build houses with foundations, but Jesus wanted them to take the same approach with his teaching, applying this practical example to a spiritual reality.

Culture, and with it the prevailing wisdom of the moment, continuously changes. If you want to keep up with it, you need to keep changing your mind about everything you thought was true. Jesus' wisdom is the rock. And, just like how a big rock stands still on a beach while the sand washes about, the wisdom of Jesus never moves; once you've heard Jesus' wisdom you can confidently stand on it knowing it's true.

But hearing wisdom is not enough. In this parable Jesus says that, once we have heard it, we need to use it like a builder uses a foundation. For instance, studying our Bibles every morning won't be any good until we apply it somehow. Going to church every Sunday and hearing great preaching won't make any difference until we start building our lives on the wisdom we hear. Even if you're preaching or reading in church, or telling everyone you know about Jesus, it *will not help you* unless you're building your own life on wisdom. Know this: we are all building *on* something, which means if you aren't building *on* wisdom you're building *on* foolishness!

So, spiritually, what does "building on" actually mean? *Building* is when *teaching* gets turned into *action*, when we start to turn wisdom into something... concrete. We "build" a life one little act at a time, each one going down like a brick on a foundation. If we approach the decisions life throws at us by praying about them and considering Jesus' teaching in a practical way, we are "building on" a firm foundation. If we don't, the chances are we'll be led by another

13

temptation, which is a bit like throwing bricks onto the sand, the way the fool did. The house we build like this will be a deathtrap in the next winter storm.

Test yourself: how well are you putting Jesus' teaching into practice? When deciding on a job, for example, do you think about how it will help your family serve the Kingdom, or follow whatever your surrounding culture tells you, which probably means taking the role that pays better? That would suggest your foundation is on the sand of wealth. Do you agree with Jesus about not committing adultery but still allow yourself lusty thoughts watching the same sexy tv drama everyone else is? Failing to build on Jesus' teaching about lust is unstable sand. Do you love to make a show of your generous giving instead of quietly serving Jesus? That's building on the sand of worldly approval. These are all subjects Jesus touches on in the sermon right before this parable…

We might have accepted the wisdom of God with our heads but have we let it into our hearts? Once it's reached our hearts it can start to move our hands! Jesus loves you, and he knows a stormy time will come when our real response to him will be exposed. So keep on seeking the true rock, digging away anything false, and putting all your weight *safely* on the true wisdom that won't collapse underneath you.

Questions for reflection:

In a storm, would you prefer to have a small house with good foundations or a huge mansion built on sand?

I once saw a photo of a house that was still standing after a massive storm; the land around it had been washed away and its foundations were exposed. How might this image encourage you in faith when facing difficult times?

What kind of things could your "sand" be? That is, what might you build your life on that might suddenly change and cause everything to collapse?

What should your firm, unmoving foundation be? Could anything move this?

One thing you can do

Keep a "foundation diary" for week – every day make a note of the things you have placed your trust in – i.e. your life's foundations. One idea is to think about how many of these things are true and solid. Are they stable enough to trust with the weight of your life?

"Not-a-Parable" of the Lawn

A friend of mine had a problem in his garden. You see, builders had been and dug up the lawn to put in a new gas tank. They'd put everything back properly, but there was this big bare patch in the middle where they'd dug. It was left flat and smooth, raked over, ready to seed; all he had to do was sow it. This situation had been left like this for weeks…

So one day, when his wife had gone into town, he says to himself, "I'm going to sort this out today." He gets up, goes to the shop and brings back a huge sack of best-quality fast-acting lawn seed, about ten times what he needed.

Arriving home, he splits open the bag and grabs a big handful of seed and lobs it into the air. Again and again, he lobs great handfuls of seed, wandering around the garden, throwing it everywhere until the whole bag is gone.

Well, some goes on the driveway and over the car, some goes in the flowerbeds, some goes in the pond, and some lands where it was needed, in the prepared ground.

The seed on the driveway blows about and gets eaten by birds. The seed in the pond water germinates but doesn't last long because it has no soil. The seed in the flowerbeds does ok for a while but it can't compete with the shrubs.

But the seed on the prepared ground went on to produce a lush, green lawn that the children and grandchildren played on. Just like it said on the packet.

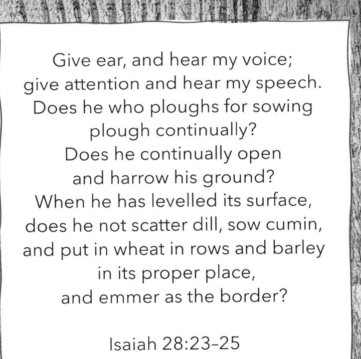

Give ear, and hear my voice;
give attention and hear my speech.
Does he who ploughs for sowing
plough continually?
Does he continually open
and harrow his ground?
When he has levelled its surface,
does he not scatter dill, sow cumin,
and put in wheat in rows and barley
in its proper place,
and emmer as the border?

Isaiah 28:23–25

2 It's All About the Soil

The Parable of the Sower

Mark 4:1-20 and Luke 8:8-15 and Matthew 13:1-23

"Listen! A Farmer went out to sow his seed. As he was scattering the seed some fell on along the path, and the birds came and ate it up. Some fell on Rocky places, where it did not have much soil. It sprang up quickly, because the soil was shallow. But when the Sun came up the plants were scorched, and they withered because they had no root. Other seed fell among thorns which grew up and choked the plants, so that they did not bear grain. Still other seed fell on good soil. It came up, grew and produced a crop, some multiplying thirty, some sixty some a hundred times." Then Jesus said, "whoever has ears to hear, let them hear."

Listen! Jesus began… Since becoming a father I have learned a few things about listening. One is that I was never really listening to my parents, or, at least, not like I thought I was. I've also realised listening – really listening – is hard. Sometimes when I speak to my children I can almost see my words hit solid ground and bouncing off unnoticed. At other times the words seem to have gained traction. But then all the enthusiasm runs out before anything gets done. Other times we get off to a good start but something colourful on a screen steals their attention. But sometimes there is real listening and there is action – those are the best days!

This is an example of how there are different types of listeners with different types of responses. In the parable, Jesus is telling us that when it comes to sharing the Gospel, your audience is likely to behave along the same lines as my children do.

I've heard it said that the Parable of the Sower warns us that 75 per cent of our efforts at sharing our faith will be wasted. I don't exactly agree with that, mostly because nothing we do faithfully for God, like preaching the Gospel, can be wasted effort, but what they meant was that you might not see the results you hoped for. What happens after the Gospel seeds are sown depends on the "soil" that the seeds land in, and that is the teaching of this parable.

The examples used by Jesus would have been very familiar to the original audience. Modern technology means that seeds can be used more sparingly and planted accurately by machine, all at the correct depth in the best prepared soil. In Jesus' day, seeds were scattered by hand – it was broadcast[8] – meaning "thrown widely". However skilled the sower was, it was still a matter of chance where each individual seed ended up. Some landed on the path where the ground was trodden down hard like concrete, some landed where weed seeds lay dormant, and some where rocks were hidden beneath the surface.

Sometimes we will be the listener, sometimes the sower, so let's think about it from both positions. First, let's put ourselves in the place of the listener. What kind of "soil" are we? Are we prepared? Are our hearts so hard that every word of God bounces right off us? Have

---

[8] Helpfully, this way of scattering seed is where the term for transmitting radio and TV is from.

we considered the rocks hidden beneath our surface?[9] What might they be? The trials; teasing from friends, the realisation we can't carry on doing "normal" things, having to give up a habit we were enjoying. When things get difficult, we will drift away if we have shallow roots.

Have we learned to pluck out the distractions and fancy things of the world[10] before they grow up and choke out the Gospel?

Now, consider the teaching from the sower's perspective: with such a low success rate it doesn't necessarily sound encouraging, does it? We usually weigh up our chances of success before we put effort into anything. (Is it worth it?) We feel discouraged if we don't see immediate results. But we are told *by Jesus* to be like the sower, *broadcasting* seeds – a generous scattering – not the sparing and calculated precision of modern planting machinery.

Jesus says that, if you've ever shared the good news with someone and it's just bounced off, don't be put off your evangelism. He told you that will happen; the ground isn't always ready. If you've seen someone struggling with their faith, they've hit difficult times, and nothing you say or pray seems to help them – don't be discouraged – Jesus said this will happen sometimes. Their roots weren't deep enough. If you've watched a young Christian get distracted, skip

---

[9] Hint: it's anything that blocks the roots of Jesus' teaching getting further into our hearts. The stoney parts of our souls that say "No further, Jesus, not here."

[10] We must learn to recognise worldly weeds for what they are – the choking riches, the smothering comforts of the world that lead us away from the truth. In medieval art the devil was always nasty-looking and evil. But in reality the devil and his temptations are very, very attractive.

church meetings and start to prioritise other things, well, Jesus told you about that too. Some seeds are trying to grow where there are too many weeds. Instead of being a total discouragement, we can see things happening just like Jesus predicted and it can strengthen our faith because we see our Lord and creator knows human hearts better than anyone.

Remember the Gospel is good seed. The different reactions aren't because of bad seeds. And it's not about the *skill* of the sower either.

It's *all about the soil.*

Our instructions are to keep telling people the good news, keep *broadcasting* the Gospel. The seeds will land in all kinds of places, we won't have precise control of where they land – but we can be assured that, once the good soil is reached, it will produce an incredible harvest of thirty, sixty or a hundred times what was sown.

Questions for reflection:

How easy do you find it to trust God with the results when you "broadcast" the good news of Jesus?

Do you trust that the seed we've been given is good seed?

What actions can you take to make sure you are being obedient to Jesus;

a) as soil?

b) as a sower?

One thing you can do

Draw up a list of friends and family who need Jesus. Start a habit of praying for them, ask God to open doors for you to share your faith with them... but also be prepared to trust God with the results!

---

3 Jesus Has Broken In

The Strong Man

Mark 3:25

And if a house is divided against itself, that house will not be able to stand. And if Satan has risen up against himself and is divided, he cannot stand; but is coming to an end. But no one can enter a strong man's house and plunder his goods, unless he first binds the strong man. Then indeed he may plunder his house.

As a child, one of the first things I was told about Jesus was that he was strong. This message was reinforced in church with songs that included the flexing biceps action. So, if you'd put me on the spot in church and asked me "Who is strong?" I would quickly reply "Jesus!" and probably I'd be on safe ground.

I love that when Jesus told this story he reversed the roles. Here the "strong man" is Satan and Jesus is a thief. Try standing up in church and asking "Who is the thief?" See if anyone shouts "Jesus!" Probably not. More likely everyone will be looking sheepish and wondering what's been stolen…

In the parables things are not always the way we expect them to be.

It might feel strange to hear Jesus describe Satan as a "strong man" but, as you walk through your town centre, who do you really feel is in control? Can you always honestly say it *feels* like Jesus is in charge?

Or sometimes does it *feel* as though Satan is? Perhaps it would depend on the day you're having. Satan *is* strong, some days it seems like Satan's winning. Perhaps that's your experience right now. Maybe you *feel* life is a constant battle. Are you struggling to "live out" your faith like you hoped to? It might *feel* as though Satan has a stronger hold on your life than Jesus does.

Does the world around you seem to laugh at God? Does it feel as though the creator is asleep, or on holiday? It might *feel* like Satan has the greatest influence on the world and people surrounding you.

Perhaps you're stuck in a cycle of temptation or sin. Satan is not ugly to us, no; in our weakness he's always tempting and attractive and ready to lure us away.

You might feel like the "strong man" Satan has you trapped in his house and there is no escape. Here is some good news: like we find in the parable, things are not always the way they *feel*. Satan *is* strong, but Jesus has broken in, he has overpowered him; Jesus has Satan tied up.

Jesus told this parable at an early stage of his ministry. The crowds were starting to get bigger. As his reputation spread, so did the resistance against him. Soon even his own family were ashamed enough to try to drag him away, saying he had gone mad. The authorities too, they announced that Jesus was possessed by Beelzebub, but this couldn't have been more wrong. Jesus is absolutely incompatible with Satan. They are completely opposed. There is no circumstance in which Jesus can work alongside Beelzebub. There is no part of the world, or time of day, or era of history where they work together. To do his work of freeing us, Jesus first restrains the devil. With the devil restrained, the raid on the house begins. Jesus steps over the threshold and Satan cannot fight back, not because he is weak but because the power of God is completely overwhelming.

Whatever sort of day you are having, Jesus has Satan tied up. Satan *is* strong, Jesus himself told us. But Jesus has already won. He is stronger, *by far*. And if you're one of his, when he comes like a thief, he will steal you away and Satan will be utterly powerless to stop him.

Questions for reflection:

Why do you think the authorities of the time wanted to suggest Jesus was in league with Satan?

What was wrong with their logic?

Does anything like this still happen today when people take a stand for Jesus? Or have we moved on?

One thing you can do

Next time you're somewhere busy, find a place to sit and watch the people around you; who is in charge of these people? Who *might* they think is in charge?

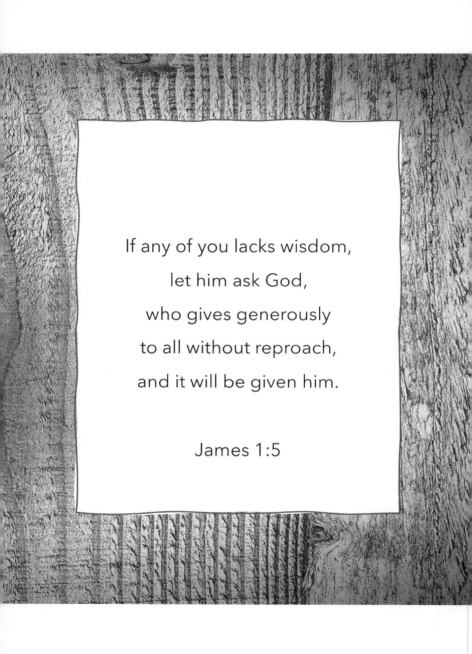

If any of you lacks wisdom,

let him ask God,

who gives generously

to all without reproach,

and it will be given him.

James 1:5

4 Let It Shine!

The Lamp on a Stand

Mark 4:21-23

And he said to them, "Is a lamp brought in to be put under a basket, or under a bed, and not on a stand? For nothing is hidden except to be made manifest; nor is anything secret except to come to light. If anyone has ears to hear, let them hear."

And he said to them, "Pay attention to what you hear: with the measure you use, it will be measured to you, and still more will be added to you. For to the one who has, more will be given, and from the one who has not, even what he has will be taken away."

Let your light shine! Or you might sometimes hear: "Don't hide your light under a bushel!" I was told that once. Not a problem, I thought to myself, I'll not make that mistake because I don't own a bushel. Or I didn't think so; at the time I didn't know what a bushel was.[11]

---

[11] For practical purposes it's a basket or bowl in this case, but I suppose that's obvious now. It was also a fixed measure of volume, which is why Jesus continued to talk about "measures". This wouldn't have needed explaining in his day...

Part one of this parable is often misused by being taken out of context. It gets used like this: "Go for it! Yeah!" "Sing your own praises", "Big yourself up and don't be shy!" It gets twisted into a worldly motivational fridge-magnet. Thankfully, knowing just the tiniest bit of context will help us understand this properly.

Just like the seeds in the Parable of the Sower, the lamp-light is the word of God, meaning true wisdom. That's what we're meant to let shine, which is quite a different thing – almost the opposite – to singing your own praises. It's about *singing God's praises*.

The image Jesus uses in this parable makes immediate sense; a light is no good to anyone smothered under a bucket. Jesus says it's just the same with the spiritual kind of light – the word of God. The purpose of that light is to shine outwards. Jesus says we weren't given it so we can hide it away. What was hidden from you is now in the open. Put that light on a stand!

Jesus continues onto part two: we are to consider what we hear (the word of God) carefully. This means to give it our full attention, to think carefully about its merits, and examine it attentively. The *measure* we use (the bushel/basket was also a kind of measure, so this was a clever link Jesus used that disappears in the English...) meaning the extent to which we do this, will be the extent to which understanding will be *measured* back to us. But generously, with extra given to us, we are promised.

I wonder if you ever sit down to read scripture and perhaps you've planned an hour but you suddenly realise you're thirty minutes in and you don't know what you've been reading. Has your mind totally wandered off onto something else? Have you reached for your smartphone? Well, that's no good at all! Jesus is telling us to give his teaching our full attention. That can't involve sitting in front of scripture daydreaming about your next business meeting or reliving a conversation you had at the school gates.

The amount of consideration and attention we invest in Jesus' teaching will be returned to us with interest. This means there is a huge reward for reading Jesus' teaching carefully, and that reward is an ever-growing knowledge of God. We will unlock enormous spiritual rewards when we diligently read and consider scripture; Jesus tells us so. Seek (understanding) and we will find (understanding). Seek the Word, find the Word.

Bringing these two parts together, both the lamp shining and our consideration of what we hear, we learn that once we have *possession of the Word of God* we are supposed to *do* something. We are to shine out – broadcasting the light to others – and engage with the Word, considering and weighing it up.

If we don't, even the little understanding we had will be taken away from us. We will become like the path in the Parable of the Sower, and the Word will bounce off us. We will be left blind, scrambling around in the dark looking for truth, but never finding it.

For me this warning rings true, and I expect it will for you as well. The amount of time we spend reading scripture and our evangelism are closely tied up. While we're in a good habit of "considering carefully what we hear" we glow with the light that refuses to be smothered. The Gospel shines out of us in a natural broadcasting of praise! But if we neglect this duty, we'll take stock one day and realise we're in the dark… under a bucket.

Questions for reflection:

If we are determined to find God's illuminating wisdom, we are promised greater understanding. How should that change our attitude to reading scripture?

If we are determined to close our hearts to God's light, we are warned that what little understanding we had will be taken away from us. How could that knowledge help us in our evangelism?

One thing you can do

Normally when we read a book - like this one - we don't get the opportunity to have the author sitting next to us helping us understand it. The Bible is different! Begin a habit of praying for understanding whenever you pick up the Bible.

5 The Coming Kingdom

The Seed Growing Secretly

Mark 4:26-29

And he said "The Kingdom of God is as if a man should scatter seed on the ground. He sleeps and rises night and day, and the seed sprouts and grows; he knows not how. The earth produces it by itself, first the blade, then the ear, then the full grain in the ear. But when the grain is ripe, at once he puts in the sickle, because the harvest has come."

Some time ago our church youth worker encouraged me and my wife to join an evangelistic sports-themed day at our local primary school.[12] Each of us had a group of children to play sport with, and teach. While we were there our group had the chance to ask us questions; it was an opportunity for them to "grill" a real live Christian – and one of the children asked me this: "Do you think it's better being a Christian, or not?" A good answer would have been "yes" but that didn't seem suitably long or profound enough. I bumbled through an answer, but I was still thinking about it the next week. Hidden in questions like that one is the idea that being a Christian is a lifestyle choice. But is faith like choosing a hobby or joining a gym, when you might try it out for a while, keeping it in the balance, to weigh up whether it works for you?

---

[12] My friends would confirm I don't have the hand-eye coordination or crowd control skills to make this a natural fit...

No. Once you've seen the truth, it's pointless weighing up whether it's better (or worse) for you than what you had before. Discipleship has a cost but you don't add it up to calculate the pros and cons.[13] To be a Christian is to be part of something mysterious, unstoppable and inevitable – the Kingdom of God.

Those who scatter the seeds of this kingdom will not be able to understand how it grows – but it will grow. That's brilliant news, because it means, like the farmer, we don't need to understand the *process*. If we're simply doing our bit, scattering seeds, then we can sleep and rise and go about our business knowing that God is on the throne over his kingdom.

However, this assuredness is never an excuse to stop thinking, or stop planning. We can't get lazy and float along expecting God to pick up the pieces. That would be a neglect of duty. We need to do our part. We *will* be called to account... but we don't need to torture ourselves about the possibility of messing up the *process* for God's growing kingdom.

And it also means it's not important we understand God's *plan* for his kingdom either. And that is fantastic news, especially when we hit what seems like a setback. When things don't go like we expected them to go it's important to know God's eternal view of events isn't the same as our view of events, nor is his plan for his kingdom the same thing as our life plans. When our church wobbles or shrinks, or a friend leaves, or our evangelism falls on deaf ears, we don't need

---

[13] In other parables Jesus encourages us to consider both the value of discipleship and the cost – see the Tower Builder and the Warring King, the Hidden Treasure and the Pearl of Great Price.

to understand why these things happen or how they fit into the big picture. Even though it's hard, we needn't doubt the Kingdom of God because something we don't understand happened.

Instead, give thanks the Kingdom of God doesn't depend on us... just the mysterious, inevitable, irrepressible, un-derailable work of God!

If you're part of the Kingdom of God, you're part of something bigger than a hobby, bigger than a lifestyle choice. You're part of something growing, mysterious and inevitable. So trust what Jesus taught in this parable, play your part without fear: the Kingdom *will* grow and the harvest *is* coming.

Questions for reflection:

How might we start to behave if we forget it is God (alone) who grows the kingdom?

On the other hand, when we remember that growing the kingdom is all God's (mysterious) work, what temptations might we fall into instead?

What would be wrong about this?

Why is it an error to think of Christianity as a mere lifestyle?

One thing you can do

Ask God for the privilege of being a part of the growth of his kingdom, then be alert for an opportunity already lined up for you; like a person you can explain your faith to, a ministry you can begin, or someone you can love better... Pray about it, and see if this seed grows...

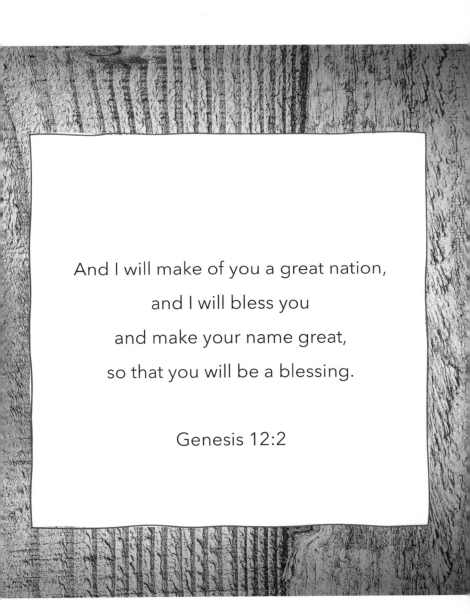

And I will make of you a great nation,

and I will bless you

and make your name great,

so that you will be a blessing.

Genesis 12:2

6 The Growing Kingdom

The Mustard Seed

Mark 4:30-32

And he said, "With what can we compare the Kingdom of God, or what parable shall we use for it? It is like a grain of mustard seed, which, when sown on the ground, is the smallest of all the seeds on earth, yet when it is sown it grows up and becomes larger than all the garden plants and puts out large branches, so that the birds of the air can make nests in its shade."

With what can we compare the Kingdom of God? Jesus asks, being rhetorical – as though to say, "You can't really compare the Kingdom of God to anything *and* it's going to be hard for you to picture the Kingdom of God but I'm going to teach you what you need to know." It's rhetorical because Jesus then immediately answers his own question in the form of a story. So right from the start we know the purpose of this new parable is to teach us more about the Kingdom of God.

Do you ever get to a church gathering and find yourself thinking that it's really small? Do you look despondently at the walls of the scruffy school hall you meet in? Do you think about your church family and sigh inwardly? Do you ever think about the way you do church and say to yourself, "This just can't be what it means to be a real part of the Kingdom of God"?

Perhaps we need to consider the mustard plant…

It's interesting that Jesus chooses a mustard plant to compare to the Kingdom of God. Not a mighty towering cedar, a formation of stars, a waterfall… with the whole of creation to choose from, there are plenty of other ideas that would be more flattering, or impressive… but a mustard plant?

Mustard seeds are pretty small. It's not that they were ever the smallest thing known to man but in Jesus' day mustard seeds were often used as an example of smallness. Like now, when we use "sliced bread" as an example of "the best thing" – even though most of us could think of several better things.[14] Mustard seeds are unremarkable; they go almost unnoticed. Yet they grow rapidly like a weed: apparently they can form a huge untidy shrub several metres wide. The mustard plant has a humble appearance, small beginnings, a distinctive flavour, and remarkable growth. It grows big enough to provide shade and shelter for birds.[15] It will attract birds from all around.

The growth of the Kingdom of God will be extraordinary, Jesus says, from tiny beginnings. Reading that now might feel comforting, but hearing it as part of Jesus' first audience would have been shocking. The rag-tag bunch of fishermen led by a teacher/carpenter from

---

[14] Which for me even includes bread that isn't sliced, but that's my subjective opinion and I'm not going to fall out with you about it.

[15] Lots of interesting things have been said about the birds. Could they represent Gentiles joining the kingdom from all around? Or even Satan roosting somehow? The safest course is to avoid allegorising details and focus on the parable's emphasis of growth – it would be a big mustard plant to take the weight of a bird.

Galilee certainly looks as small and unimpressive as a mustard seed. But surely he can't be claiming his new kingdom will become something huge? This man is deluded, they might think. Jumped up and overconfident.

But look how it's turned out so far. It's worth remembering that, although Jesus started out with a few fishermen on a beach, today he has more followers than anyone on Instagram; in fact, it's thought there are seven times more believers now than people on the planet in AD 1.

Sometimes being part of the Kingdom of God isn't like we might have hoped or expected. So if you ever find yourself thinking the way you do church is messy, or if you find yourself wondering if Jesus had pictured something grander, or wondering if something small or tangled can be an important part of God's kingdom... don't be discouraged.

Remember, given the whole of creation to pick from, the mustard plant is what Jesus chose to compare his kingdom to. The proverbially small seed nobody notices, capable of incredible growth into something unbelievably massive.

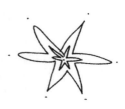

Questions for reflection:

Does your church feel more like part of a cedar of Lebanon or a mustard bush?

How do you think Jesus' disciples felt, hearing Jesus offer these predictions of the future?

What does this parable mean for the future of the Church of Christ?

One thing you can do

Jesus' audience was very familiar with the basics of farming, but these days some of us are quite removed from this. If that's you, plant a few seeds and watch them grow; you can remind yourself about the mustard plant Jesus talked about while it gets bigger.

The Pharisees came and began to argue
with him, seeking from him a sign
from heaven to test him.

And he sighed deeply in his spirit and
said, "Why does this generation
seek a sign? Truly, I say to you,
no sign will be given to this generation."

And he left them,
got into the boat again,
and went to the other side.

Mark 8:11-13

7 Some Won't Listen

The Children in the Marketplace

Luke 7:31-35

To what shall I compare the people of this generation, and what are they like? They are like children sitting in the marketplace and calling to one another; "We played the flute for you, and you did not dance; we sang a dirge, and you did not weep." For John the Baptist has come eating no bread and drinking no wine, and you say, "He has a demon." The Son of Man has come eating and drinking, and you say, "Look at him! A glutton and a drunkard, a friend of tax collectors and sinners!" Yet wisdom is justified by her children.

In a park one afternoon, I watched a small child pull off his hat and throw it on the ground. Then they started crying because their hat was gone. So their mother put it back on the child's head. But this wasn't right either; more tears came. The hat was thrown off... better? No. It was upsetting and there were more tears. The hat went back on. Worse. There was no pleasing this child. I began to think, "This isn't about the hat..."

In Luke, Chapter 7, we read that John the Baptist had sent two of his followers to Jesus, to ask if he really was the Messiah – or if they should wait for someone else. When they arrived Jesus was surrounded by a crowd, as usual, busy with his daily ministry. Jesus answered by telling them to take a look around: "The blind receive their sight, the lame walk, lepers are cleansed, the deaf hear, the dead are raised up, the poor have good news preached to them. And blessed is the one who is not offended by me." It seems like this was enough of an answer for them – with all his miracles and preaching, Jesus was already answering the prophecies in the scriptures. John's followers headed home confident that they had found the right man.

Many people in Jesus' crowd would also have heard of John the Baptist. But, even though they were cousins, born only six months apart, John had a very different public image to Jesus. John lived in the wilderness outside the city walls and he wore rough, itchy camel-hair clothes – like the olden-day prophets had. Instead of meat and wine, he fasted regularly, and the rest of the time lived off wild insects and honey. John was announcing the coming Messiah. He was warning everyone that – for all their waiting – they simply weren't ready yet, so he called his followers to turn away from their sins, now, and be baptised in the river in preparation. It was a tough message of sin, failure, unpreparedness and coming judgement... which is why his ministry was compared to a funeral.

Jesus, on the other hand, healed people. He corrected blindness, lameness and even death. He drank wine (he even supplied it on at least one occasion!) and went to dinners with temple leaders. He reached out to everyone – including the dark fringes of society like the sex workers and the hated tax collectors.[16] Compared to John's ministry, Jesus' looked more like a wedding.

---

[16] It's hard to imagine just how much everyone hated the tax collectors... but it was *a lot*.

After John's followers left, Jesus turns to the crowd and tells them this parable. In the story, one group of children played their flutes for another group but no one danced. They sang a sad song but no one cried. Neither the happy music nor the sad song was right for them.

It was like that for Jesus and John. They lived very different lifestyles but some people still found reasons to reject them both. John fasted, so people said he was possessed and they rejected his message of repentance. Jesus ate, drank and spoke to the sinful, so they said he was a drunk and they rejected him for the opposite reason.

Their inconsistency revealed their insincerity – it wasn't really about Jesus' (or John's) lifestyle at all! Jesus pointed to the real issue: a pig-headed determination to reject his message, at whatever cost. With some people you will never win.

Many of those who followed Jesus and John were the *outcasts* of society: the poor, the publicans, tax collectors, recognised "sinners". On the other side were the rejecters, made up of the self-righteous Pharisees, lawyers, leaders of the temple cult.[17] For the *in-crowd* people, Jesus' message of a dawning new kingdom was unwelcome. Despite the fact they'd been waiting for the Messiah for generations, it turned out the Messiah was the very last person they wanted to see right then. For the *in-crowd*, the last thing they wanted was for Jesus to be exactly who he said he was, and to come and steal their

---

[17] They were self-righteous in the sense that they had set rules for righteousness and were meticulous in keeping them. Thus they believed they were right with God and didn't need further intervention.

limelight and put them in their places. Just as they had rejected John's baptism, they were rejecting Jesus too.

Life, for the *in-crowd*, was too good to have anyone rocking the boat. Jesus and John were challenging them, and they would have said *anything* it took, however inconsistent, to make the challenge go away. By calling Jesus a drunk, they didn't need to worry about his claim to be the son of God. So they didn't need to carefully examine his teaching, and they didn't need to confront their sin, or their coming judgement. They could get back to their comfortable lives surrounded by people who said comfortable things.

Jumbled-up priorities were the error of the rejecters. They were enjoying what they had *here and now*, and it was more important to them than *eternity*. It's like refusing to leave the airport lounge – even though you're about to miss your flight. They chose temporary *comfort* over uncomfortable *truth*.

We need to be careful of this too, because our hearts are the same. The more comfortable we are, the harder it is to hear Jesus. We can refuse to recognise truth, however it is presented. Is there some *particular* teaching that you would rather tie yourself in knots to argue away, because you already decided not to hear it? If so, it's probably because it's the one with the most unwelcome news for you.

So are you ever behaving like these children in the marketplace? I'm not going to dance, and you can't make me cry. He's just a drunk, and his cousin was possessed...

Jesus ends on a little note, "yet wisdom is justified by her children", which simply means that in time it will become obvious who was right. In the end, it will be important who we rejected and who we listened to.

Questions for reflection:

Why do you think John's followers, and John himself, wanted confirmation from Jesus about his identity as Messiah?

How do we respond to those who are determined to reject the good news of the Kingdom?

In Mark 8:11–13 Jesus refused to give a "sign" – why do you think that might be?

What are the implications of "wisdom is justified by her children"?

One thing you can do

Our addiction to comfort often stops us short in our discipleship. Commit to do something (for God's kingdom) that you'd normally avoid because it *makes you uncomfortable*.

8 Who Will Be Grateful?

The Two Debtors

Luke 7:40-43

And Jesus answering said to him "Simon, I have something to say to you." And he answered "Say it, Teacher."

"A certain moneylender had two debtors. One owed five hundred denarii, and the other fifty. When they could not pay he cancelled the debt of both. Now which of them will love him more?" Simon answered, "The one, I suppose, for whom he cancelled the larger debt." And he said to him, "You have judged rightly."

Jesus was well known for speaking out against the religious leaders of his day. Despite that, in Luke we find out that a Pharisee, Simon, has invited him into his home to eat a meal with him and his friends. Perhaps he had heard Jesus teaching in the synagogue earlier in the day and, impressed by what he heard (notice: "Say it, Teacher"), invited him for a sabbath meal. Showing hospitality to travelling teachers was the *right thing* to do back then. It was *meritorious* and would have reflected well on Simon.

On that night, while Jesus was there, a local woman turned up in Simon's home.[18] She got behind Jesus. Her tears running down her

---

[18] Perhaps this woman had also heard Jesus teaching earlier, and we might guess the teaching was about forgiveness?

cheeks and wetting his feet, she let out her hair to wipe them. She kissed each foot and rubbed them with perfumed ointment.

It's fairly hard to imagine how this strange scene would be received. If it happened today it would be odd enough. But, in the culture of the time, there's even more going on here to make it extraordinary. For a start, feet were unclean.[19] To *wash* somebody's grubby feet demonstrated you were a servant. To *kiss* a person's feet showed gratitude and humility, as though you're addressing a king who had spared your life. A woman's hair was not usually on show when men were around, never mind being used as a towel... on feet.

Being a Pharisee, our host, Simon, has a keenly trained eye for anything or anyone unclean.[20] He zoomed in on the fact that this woman wasn't a clean woman but a sinner, which probably means a prostitute. Simon thought to himself: if Jesus really were a prophet, he'd have spotted the woman was a sinner. If Simon had been in Jesus' position, perhaps he would have pushed her away and sent her back into the street. We aren't told.

Whatever Simon might have done, Jesus accepted her. And he knew a great deal more about this woman than our Pharisee could ever have guessed at.

For her part – she knew her life was corrupt, her spiritual condition was a mess, and yet she was offered forgiveness for it all. She was

---

[19] Both ceremonially *and* literally from the dusty streets. Modern feet still aren't very nice; we haven't moved on.
[20] He needed one, so that he could spot who to avoid. "Pharisee" literally means "separatist" or "one who is separated".

overflowing with gratitude and, as we watch her, overwhelmed, she pours out her love, like the ointment from her alabaster jar.

Then, with all this going on at his feet, Jesus addressed Simon with a question, in the form of a simple parable. There are two people owing money, one more, one less. Both are forgiven; which loves the forgiver more? Simon answered that it's the one forgiven more. He must have realised, watching the woman now kissing Jesus' feet, that he, Simon the Pharisee, was the less grateful man. This prostitute was closer to God than Simon was. She had something right that Simon had wrong.

The mistake of the Pharisees (in general) was to trust in their own goodness, that if they did the right things and followed the right rules it made them righteous, and therefore better than the world around them. We must remember in our natural state there is nothing very different about the heart of a Pharisee than the rest of us. We all (rightly) agree when someone says we're all sinners. But we still love the idea that some of us have a better handle on sin, enough to *earn* God's respect and salvation. Christians can do that very easily...

Do I, *having come to Christ*, now think I'm better than other people? Do I, *having come to Christ*, now look down on other people who join the church who don't appear to be as squeaky clean as I believe I am? Do I, *having come to Christ*, think I'm *more* forgiven than other Christians, because they were forgiven for *more* than I was?

Jesus is teaching that God can forgive us whatever our spiritual state, but it will be those who understand their debt who will respond with love and gratitude. If we remember the enormous debt we were forgiven, we can live rightly *in loving gratitude* to the one who forgave us.

Questions for reflection:

Why do you think it's so tempting to forget, or play down, the debt we have been forgiven by Jesus?

But why might this be a terrible thing to do?

How can we fight off this temptation and remain grateful to God?

One thing you can do

In private, write down on paper (this is to help you commit to it) the worst thing you can remember ever *being forgiven for*. Pray to God for thanks!

(Now you can destroy the paper)

"Not-a-Parable" of the Riot

In London, summer 2020 saw a series of protests and counter-protests following each other. These led to violent riots breaking out, as different groups met on the streets to represent their different causes, and the police fought to separate and control them. On one occasion, with events getting out of hand, amid the smoke grenades and flying bottles, this story unfolded.

A drunk and disorientated far-right protestor had become separated from his group, and found himself caught up within a Black Lives Matter (BLM) protest. Given that tensions were already running high, this was a dangerous place to be.

With the man surrounded and being beaten, Patrick Hutchinson (with the BLM protest), saw this happening and said, "He was under physical harm, his life was under threat. And I thought, well, if he stays here he's not going to make it." So he hoisted the man onto his shoulders and carried him through the crowds to the police line.

Despite being on opposing sides of the riot, Patrick Hutchinson is widely credited with saving the life of this far-right protestor, who had been separated by his group.

Who was the neighbour to the beaten man?

9 Who Is My Neighbour?

The *Good* Samaritan

Luke 10:25-37

Jesus replied, "A man was going down from Jerusalem to Jericho, and he fell among robbers, who stripped him and beat him and departed, leaving him half dead. Now by chance a priest was going down that road and when he saw him he passed by on the other side. So likewise a Levite, when he came to the place and saw him, passed by on the other side. But a Samaritan, as he journeyed, came to where he was, and when he saw him, he had compassion. He went to him and bound up his wounds, pouring on oil and wine. Then he set him on his own animal and brought him to an inn and took care of him. And the next day he took out two denarii and gave them to the innkeeper, saying, "Take care of him, and whatever more you spend, I will repay you when I come back." Which of these three, do you think, proved to be a neighbour to the man who fell among the robbers?"

The biblical law to love our neighbour as ourselves was well known and, in fact, an expert in religious law had just quoted it to Jesus. But when he asked Jesus who his neighbour was, the answer came in a surprising parable of violence, neglect and love. It was followed by a question: who was the neighbour to *this* man?

Since this is one of the most well known of Jesus' parables, we probably miss how explosive it would have been at the time! These days we have a charity named after the Samaritans, and the word "Samaritan" is so closely associated with "good" that it's hard to separate them. If someone says "Samaritan", someone else will be thinking "good". But in Jesus' day they were opposites. Like a delightful tax bill or some welcome nausea or a happy traffic jam. A *good* Samaritan would have been the kind of surprise that has an interesting story behind it... or, in this case, an interesting parable...

So who were these Samaritans and why were they so disliked? Well, these people were descendants of the northern tribes of Israel, who broke away in the wars after Solomon's death. They had set up their own places of worship,[21] interfered with scripture, and intermarried with the local pagans, all of which made them traitors. In the eyes of the Jerusalem Jews they were revolting and corrupt. This is why Jews and Samaritans hated each other. They treated each other's cities and towns as unclean, and would take routes that avoided crossing each other's paths.

The priest and the Levite, on the other hand, were heroes of their day. Their cleanliness and godliness were unquestioned and their attitude to keeping God's law was admirable.

Quite intentionally, Jesus has made this story an *uncomfortable surprise*. It's *uncomfortable* because these people wouldn't normally want to even be near each other. If he had been conscious it's possible he'd have told the Samaritan to go away and leave him to die. It's *surprising* because the good guys – the priest and Levite – left the victim for

---

[21] Instead of returning to the Jerusalem temple like they were supposed to.

dead. Yet the Samaritan showed love. It's *surprising* because an enemy can still be a neighbour.

How do we apply the lesson of the good Samaritan today?

Firstly, to have a box-ticking, legalistic view of God's law is a mistake. This is the attitude behind the original question posed – "And who is my neighbour?" – Or "Please Jesus, define the legal *limits* within which you would have us love each other!" For the priest and Levite, their preoccupation with the temple, grand ideas about their religious status and a desire for cleanliness (which trumped even love) led them to leave one of God's covenant children bleeding in the dust. An obsession with keeping to the fine points of temple regulations had resulted in a lack of compassion and blinded them to the *first and second commandments.*[22]

Secondly, Jesus' definition of neighbourhood bridges social division. The Samaritan and the Jew were from opposing cultures who traditionally hated each other. Nevertheless, in Jesus' story the Samaritan reaches across this division to help someone in need, and by doing this he keeps *the covenant commandment* to "love his neighbour". The generations of hatred could have excused him for not helping – nobody would have judged him for it – but this man acted in love.

Thirdly, loving your neighbour applies to us all. There isn't a status you can rise to that lets you off the hook. Religious order, like being a vicar or a pastor or a priest, or becoming rich or popular, or having a celebrated talent... none of this means God puts you beyond

---

[22] ... on which all the other laws hang...

loving your neighbour. Church membership doesn't mean you can ignore the homeless on the road outside. As a commandment of God, *loving your neighbour* trumps all the inconvenience and difficulty that might arise from putting it into practice. And, if we're being honest, it usually is both inconvenient and difficult.

Finally, your neighbour might also be your enemy. There is nobody so vile and revolting, nobody so hated and disgusting that they don't count. Nobody so infuriating on social media, so bitterly set against your faith, so aggressively anti-Christian, so drug-addicted that when you find them in distress you don't need to pick them up, dust them off and follow the example of the Samaritan.

God has shown compassion to another rebellious sinner; that person is you. You were once an enemy of God, yet he showed you mercy.

As Jesus said, "You go, and do likewise" (Luke 10:37).

Questions for reflection:

Does Jesus set limits on who our neighbour is?

To love our neighbour we need to understand who our neighbour is but also what love is. How is love different to kindness, affirmation or just being nice?

Does loving your neighbour require liking your neighbour?

Might loving your neighbour sometimes involve disagreeing with them?

One thing you can do

Agree to help someone out in some practical way. It might something be big or small but offer it to someone you wouldn't normally hang around with.

(Ask God to set you up!)

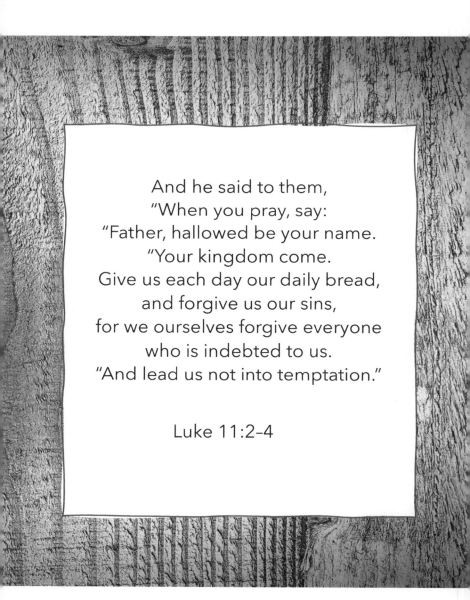

And he said to them,
"When you pray, say:
"Father, hallowed be your name.
"Your kingdom come.
Give us each day our daily bread,
and forgive us our sins,
for we ourselves forgive everyone
who is indebted to us.
"And lead us not into temptation."

Luke 11:2-4

10 Ask Me for Anything

The Friend at Midnight

Luke 11:5-8

And he said to them, "Which of you who has a friend will go to him at midnight and say to him 'Friend, lend me three loaves, for a friend of mine has arrived on a journey, and I have nothing to set before him'; and he will answer from within, 'Do not bother me; the door is now shut, and my children are with me in bed. I cannot get up and give you anything'? I tell you, though he will not get up and give him anything because he is a friend, yet because of his impudence he will rise and give him whatever he needs."

Has a friend ever asked you for help with something, that was actually going to be really inconvenient? Almost everyone you ask can tell you about a time they were put in this position – but agreed anyway.[23] As an example, not long ago someone asked me to help move a few things from his garage. It wasn't a convenient time. I didn't want to do it, and I quickly discovered we had very different ideas about what *a few things* really means. But he needed the help and I agreed to do it.

---

[23] Almost everyone – if you're one of the people who can't, you're probably asking too much from your friends...

As always, if we want to learn the lesson of this parable we need to pay attention to the context. One of the disciples had just asked Jesus to teach them to pray – because John the Baptist had taught his students to pray. This parable comes right in the middle of his answer, telling us the subject is prayer. So Jesus isn't teaching us about hospitality, sharing food or getting up at midnight. This interesting little parable is about our attitude in prayer.

The plot reminds us that some things haven't changed; being asked for something inconvenient is a timeless problem. A few things have changed, though, especially technology. I mention this because arriving somewhere without bread might sound trivial to our modern ears. But travel took a lot longer on a donkey (no cars) and there was no way to phone ahead in those days (no phones) and food was harder to store (no freezers) or purchase at night (no twenty-four-hour petrol stations), so this travelling friend will have arrived in need of food. And this is an important point when we start to think about what the parable means: the bread he asked for was something he needed; it wasn't just something he fancied the look of, or idolised.

It's also worth getting our heads into a cultural difference between then and now. Today, particularly in the west, we generally think of ourselves as individuals. We live in small, quite isolated families, we think a lot about our personal identity. We talk a lot about "me" and "I". This is the influence of our culture. When anything happens, our first and most natural reaction is to think about how that affects us as individuals. Whenever we do something, we consider how it will reflect on ourselves. This has been called an individualistic culture.

Back in Jesus' time the culture was less focussed on the individual and more about the group, and group identity would have been a more natural way of thinking about yourself. This has been described as a culture of honour and shame. The good things they did brought honour to their families, honour to their community and honour to God. The bad things they did brought shame on themselves and shame on their communities.

In both cultures we might help each other out of a fix – but why we do it and the way we think about our actions might be rather different. Let's consider that now…

When Jesus began a parable with the phrase "Which of you…?" his way of putting it showed he expected his audience to know the answer. It is a rhetorical question, meaning, "None of you has a friend who – when this happens – would turn you away empty-handed." So the expectation of this culture is that anyone in those circumstances would provide bread, even when asked at midnight after they locked the house up.[24] Your neighbourhood might be like that, but it might not! If you want to find out I suggest you set your alarm for the small hours and get out there knocking on doors. If you do, let me know how it goes.

The reason he can count on this neighbour is spelled out in the parable: it's not because it's a friend asking, and it can't be because the request is welcome, or because the bread is deserved. No, it is because of his "impudence", the shamelessness of his request at such a late hour. The original audience would have been sensitive to the

---

[24] Even when this meant clambering over everyone in the small house, or waking the children up with a noisy door bolt…

shame of not having food to offer, and the honour to his household by providing the bread needed to the friend. It was shameful to the whole community if you didn't offer hospitality. All of these thoughts would have been in the minds of Jesus' audience as he told them this parable.

The lesson Jesus wants to teach us about prayer is this: if a tired and grumpy friend, woken up in the night, can still be depended on when you need them, then how much more will God (who is neither grumpy nor tired) help his children when they ask for what they need? In fact, incredibly, since we are adopted by God and part of his community, it somehow brings honour to God when he answers the prayers of believers – in the same way it did for the woken man to lend bread to his friend in that community.

In prayer we should approach God for what we need. We can approach God boldly, without shame, for things we don't necessarily deserve. And there isn't a bad time to ask – we don't need to hesitate to ask God for the things he has promised us.

We mustn't carry the idea that our Lord is a distant king, uninterested in the daily needs of his subjects. We are his children, living in communion with him. He delights in the details of our lives and overlooks nothing. He is honoured to help us and pleased to hear from us, so, if you need it, pray for it boldly.

Questions for reflection:

Think of an unreasonable request you made to a friend or even stranger. What made you so bold?

We are invited to pray to our Lord without shame. What might stop us from doing this wholeheartedly?

Is there any time that God would find it inconvenient to hear a prayer from us?

One thing you can do

Pray! Do it a time of day or night you've never prayed before. Do it knowing God is still listening.

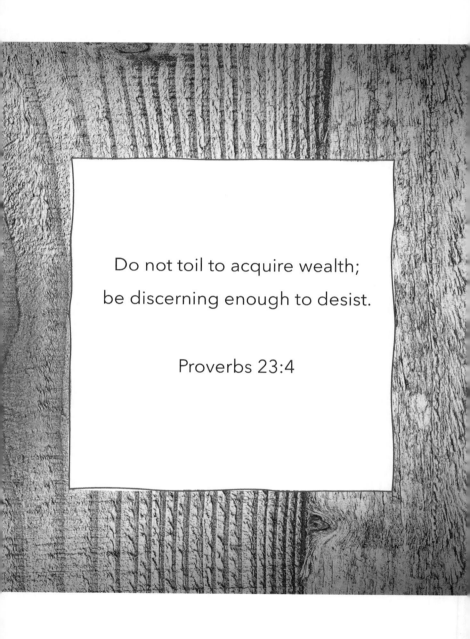

Do not toil to acquire wealth;

be discerning enough to desist.

Proverbs 23:4

"Not-a-Parable" of the Grand Design

On the route between our house and our children's school there was a small bungalow, on a large plot of land. Our children were in their first year of school when it was sold to a wealthy couple from London. Having inherited a lot of money, they were planning a retirement in the country.

"We will live a life of luxury!" the husband said to his wife. They submitted plans to build a huge mansion in place of the bungalow.

They moved into a small room above the garage while the bungalow was demolished, and work began. But the work did not go smoothly. By the time our children were in year three, the project had still barely started. As our children reached their final year in school, our daily commute was still taking us past a muddy and messy building site. The retired couple were still living above their garage in that small room.

Suddenly, stress taking its toll, and with the project still going slowly, the husband died.

Who is going to enjoy the mansion now?

11 The Man Who Had Everything

The Rich Fool

Luke 12:13-21

The ground of a certain rich man yielded an abundant harvest. He thought to himself, "What shall I do? I have no place to store my crops." Then he said, "This is what I'll do. I will tear down my barns and build bigger ones, and there I will store my surplus grain. And I'll say to myself, 'You have plenty of grain laid up for many years. Take life easy; eat, drink and be merry.'" But God said to him, "You fool! This very night your life will be demanded from you. Then who will get what you have prepared for yourself?" This is how it will be with whoever stores up things for themselves but is not rich towards God.

There is a certain romance about exploring the stately homes of England. They are lovely places, many of them are kept carefully restored, along with their beautiful gardens, so that families can come and see them – for a small fee.[25] They are relics of a bygone age, a seemingly simpler time of mud, horses, feudalism and servitude. They are also *one* answer to a question that certain

---

[25] Or, in some cases, for quite a large fee.

people[26] have been asking in every civilisation since sin began. "What shall I do with this excess I have?" The pyramids of Egypt, the palaces and arenas of Rome, the solid gold guns of Saddam Hussain, the supercars, yachts and spaceships of today... they all offer an answer to the same question. "I have nowhere to store my crops."

To be rich means to have more than you need. The man in this parable started off that way: he was a rich man. Yet now the ground had produced an abundant harvest for him. Jesus reminds us that this plentiful crop came up from *the ground*. Like everything we own, it was a generous gift from God. But this gift posed a problem; already having an abundance, the man had nothing to do with it.

This being the case, he thought, "I will build bigger stores and fill them with my surplus grain. And I will live in luxury." But God stepped in and called him a fool, then told him his life was over and somebody else would get this grain.

The rich man was clearly in error; but what exactly was his error? Are we off the hook if we aren't rich enough to own a yacht? And what does it mean to be *rich towards God*? These are all good questions, so let's try to answer them.

Firstly, we consider the error. Jesus gave this parable in public; it was an answer to a man in the crowd who asked him to help with an inheritance dispute. Jesus declined, and warned the crowd, "Take care, and be on your guard against all covetousness, for one's life does not consist in the abundance of his possessions." So the error

---

[26] Rich people.

this parable is warning against is materialism,[27] which is the belief that material *things* are what life is about. The rich man had a materialistic belief system that was revealed by his behaviour.

For the follower of materialism, life is about your *things* and so the only valid thing to do with a surplus is to store it up to increase your comfort, or buy some more *things*. This is greedy, selfish... and extremely popular. Jesus warns us to "take care and be on our guard" for a very good reason: we are all ready to slip into this behaviour. Whether it's a spaceship or a chocolate bar, the temptation is to want *and* keep more than we need. So no, sadly, we are not let off the hook if we don't own a yacht.

To motivate us, this parable exposes materialism to be a flimsy foundation for building a life on. In the end, for all the luxury and security the rich man's wealth afforded him on earth, it didn't provide any protection when God took away his life. Someone else would get to eat his grain, drink his wine and live in his house. The rich man had given his heart[28] to the pursuit of *things*, but these *things* offered him nothing in return when it mattered.

By contrast, being "rich towards God" involves living with wisdom, following Jesus' advice about steering yourself away from material covetousness. It means putting your heart in heaven and building up eternal treasure where it will actually be of eternal use to you. It is

---

[27] Materialism – to consider possessions and physical comfort more important than spiritual things.
[28] "For where your treasure is, there your heart will be also" (Matthew 6:21).

where our heart is that matters, and where our heart is, will be revealed by what we do with our abundances.

It has been said, wisely, that if you want to know what someone believes, look at what they do with their money. I suggest we challenge ourselves by considering our finances and seeing what our money is saying about us. Perhaps do an annual assessment. What you spend, particularly when you have more than you need, reveals what you worship in practice; would you find evidence of Jesus in your bank account? Or is it all coffee shops, a thirsty car and holidays?

In this explosive parable Jesus has thrown out a massive challenge and a powerful warning. We often describe our time as a materialistic age but I'm not convinced we're living through anything new; all ages have been materialistic. Around each stately home in England there were, I suspect, plenty of servants dreaming of the high life. It isn't material success[29] Jesus warns us about here but the covetousness and pursuit of material things, and the belief that *things* are what life is about.

Make sure you're putting your money where your heart is and building up treasure in heaven. Be rich towards God.

---

[29] Although material success will make things harder (Mark 10:25).

Questions for reflection:

The rich fool must have had other options to steward his abundant harvest — what might they have been?

Where do our wealth and possessions really come from?

Just before this parable Jesus warned the crowd, "Life does not consist in an abundance of possessions." Why do you think it's so common to chase after an abundance instead of stewarding what we have been given?

What advice should a Christian give a person who is trapped in materialistic thought?

One thing you can do

Challenge your materialism by finding one thing in your home to give away. It should be something you're "attached" to. If you can't think of something, be brave, and ask God to reveal it to you in his own time...

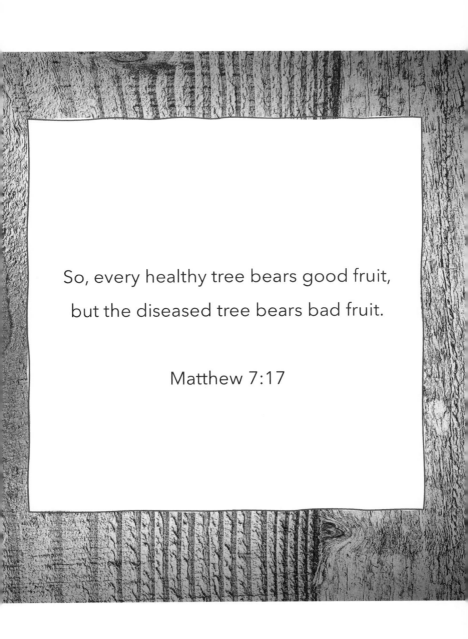

So, every healthy tree bears good fruit,

but the diseased tree bears bad fruit.

Matthew 7:17

12 Growing Fruit

The Barren Fig Tree

Luke 13:6-9

And He told this parable: "A man had a fig tree planted in his vineyard, and he came seeking fruit on it and found none. And he said to the vinedresser, 'Look, for three years now I have come seeking fruit on this fig tree, and I find none. Cut it down. Why should it use up the ground?' And he answered him, 'Sir, let it alone this year also, until I dig around it and put on manure. Then if it should bear fruit next year, well and good; but if not, you can cut it down.'"

O ur family sometimes grows tomatoes in a greenhouse, and that's what we tell people.[30] We don't say we're hoping to grow bushy, green-stemmed things in growbags; people would – rightly – wonder what was going on. We say, "We're growing tomatoes" because the *purpose* of growing tomato plants is having fresh tomatoes we can eat. The same goes for any harvest. The *purpose* of a fruit tree is obvious: it's fruit. Understandably, the owner of the vineyard wanted figs when he planted a fig tree. If the tree doesn't give him any fruit, why should it take up the soil?

---

[30] Only if it comes up in conversation. We don't push this information on people.

So this fig tree needs to repent or it's going to get destroyed. If it remains a useless waste of good soil, its place in the vineyard is not something to take for granted.

Jesus told this parable in the context of:

- Readiness (Luke 12:35: "Stay dressed for action and keep your lamps burning").
- Coming judgement on the horizon (Luke 12:54: "When you see a cloud coming in the west, you say at once 'A shower is coming'").
- The need to repent before the coming judgement (Luke 13:4: "Those eighteen on whom the tower in Siloam fell and killed them: do you think they were worse offenders than all the others who lived in Jerusalem? No, I tell you; but unless you repent, you will all likewise perish").

Familiar with scripture, Jesus' first audience would have known the vineyard was a symbol for the Kingdom of God, and hence the vineyard owner was God. The barren fig tree that is spared for another year represents the Jews of Jesus' day. Fruit would be some kind of output of their faith – but it can be visible in all sorts of forms.

The message is clear. God is patient; he has been waiting. Right now he's still waiting, while graciously providing for his people. But the people of God show themselves by how they act, and without that they cannot say they have a place in the kingdom. A day is coming when God's patience will run out; those who don't belong will be cut down like a fruitless tree.

Jesus was calling time on the fruitless temple culture.

What does this mean for us? How do we respond?

Some of us might need to hear that God is patient and graceful, not immediately dishing out the judgement we deserve. This is a good thing! All of us sin and miss the mark. But during our fruitless years we have all still benefitted from his care and provision. Each day we wake up, breathe air, drink water, eat food and wonder at the abundant beauty of creation. This is what gets called "common grace" – because it's available to everyone.

But the end is coming. Our time of common grace is running out. We have to face the facts: our life is finite and judgement will catch up with us sooner or later.[31] Like the fig tree, we'd better be caught with at least a little fruit to show for our place in the Kingdom. It's not good enough to be living *near* fruit, or *look like* fruit, or *smell like* fruit, or *know somebody* who once made a lot of fruit. We need to show some of our own, and it will be in accordance with the type of tree we are, and where we've been planted.

Being a part of a fruitful church, for instance, isn't going to be enough unless you're contributing to the harvest. This might be hard for us to hear. Be glad God has given us a time of grace to wait for us, but don't waste this time by being inactive.

This isn't *salvation by works*. Your works can't buy your life, we are saved by faith. But just like how a good tree, in the right soil, can't

---

[31] Some take this parable to point towards the coming end of all time, while others see our individual mortality, but in terms of how we respond it hardly matters. Either one of those ends could happen to us today.

help revealing itself by its fruit, saving faith can be seen by the life you live. Fruit hanging on the branches is evidence of healthy roots.

If this parable is making you feel a bit wobbly, pay attention to your roots. Build those roots up; consider how you need to change or grow. Dig in some nourishment like the parable suggests for the fig tree. Not literal manure, though – instead, the habits of prayer and reading scripture – and be certain you're in a vineyard – a healthy Christian fellowship – and actively look for opportunities to use your particular gifts to serve that community. You will be astonished how God can use healthy, well rooted believers.

Questions for reflection:

Why is God such a patient gardener? Do we deserve this grace?

What will it look like to be a tree cut down and removed from the vineyard?

Think of some examples of "fruit" in your life.

One thing you can do

Do a "stock check" on your fruitfulness. Thinking back over the last year – or more – how have your prayer life, biblical knowledge, habits, love and obedience to God grown? Are you growing fruit for the kingdom?

Part 2

The Gathering Clouds

The Approach to Jerusalem

Jesus uses parables to teach about his Kingdom; including its value, cost, membership and mission.

"Not-a-Parables" of the Runner and the Homebuyer

Would any of you turn up to run a marathon without planning it first? Before you agreed to it you'd think about your training, and get all the right kit, like running shoes. Otherwise, you'd get halfway round and run out of breath. People would make fun of you, saying, "She hasn't thought this through; she has started something she cannot finish!"

Who would agree to buy a house with a mortgage, without making sure they can afford the monthly payments? First you sit down with a calculator and make sure you're confident. If you're not, you need to pull out before it's too late. Otherwise, you could lose your home and you, along with your family, will be living on the street.

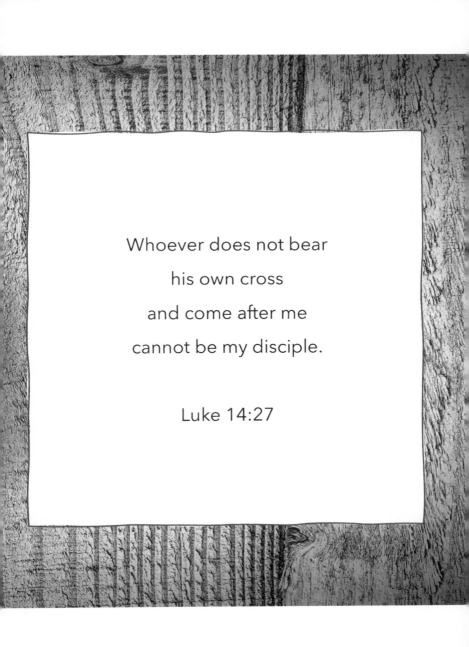

Whoever does not bear

his own cross

and come after me

cannot be my disciple.

Luke 14:27

13 Discipleship Will Have a Cost

The Tower Builder and Warring King

Luke 14:28-33

For which of you, desiring to build a tower, does not first sit down and count the cost, whether he has enough to complete it? Otherwise, when he has laid a foundation and is not able to finish, all who see it begin to mock him, saying, "This man began to build and was not able to finish." Or what king, going out to encounter another king in war, will not sit down first and deliberate whether he is able with ten thousand to meet him who comes against him with twenty thousand? And if not, while the other is yet a great way off, he sends a delegation and asks for terms of peace. So therefore, any one of you who does not renounce all that he has cannot be my disciple.

When the government announced the national Covid lockdown in England, my wife and I made a decision that felt brave. We decided to push ahead with building a garage like we had planned, even though we'd no longer be able to use the tradesmen and contractors that we had intended to. As the foundations were being poured, someone handed me a rake, and I had to admit that I'd never done this before, and I didn't know what

I was supposed to do next. Some of my friends found it funny to remind me of this parable. Perhaps *I* would become the parable: the man who had begun to build but was not able to finish.

The truth was, even though it was going to be a steep learning curve, we *had* sat down and counted the cost. We knew it would be hard work, and it was going to be expensive, and there were lots of unknowns too. But we weighed it up and decided we would have enough energy and money to finish it – and we were ready to learn whatever else we needed to as we went along.[32]

In these parables, Jesus says the builder counts the cost to see if he can afford it. Not whether it's expensive or hard to do, or risky... the important question is: did the builder *think about it* first and start off with his *eyes open*? When Jesus asks, "For which of you...?" he means "Surely nobody would...?"

Because nobody would start a building project *before* considering if they can finish it. A half-finished building would be a permanent monument to their stupidity. Nobody wants that. Most of us, and I include myself in this, are perfectly capable of showing our stupidity without building everyone a big reminder...

In the case of the king, Jesus says he would *consider* if he can win, given the numbers are stacked against him. The king considers his chances of survival *before* the battle. Can I win this war if the enemy outnumbers me two to one? Or do I need to negotiate now before

---

[32] As it happens, I'm writing this in the upstairs room of the garage we finished... It was hard to build but, yes, it was worth it!

it's too late? He needs to engage his brain first, and plan what to do. Again, the message is open-eyed *consideration*.

Notice the stakes are higher for the king than for the builder: if the builder can't finish his project he'll look stupid, but the king stands to lose his army, his kingdom and – most probably – his life. Then Jesus concludes by saying anyone who isn't prepared to "renounce all he has" can't be one of his disciples. This raises the stakes another notch: now we risk discipleship, the Kingdom of God and everlasting life.

So the meaning is clear; given that the cost of discipleship *will* be high, we must enter it thoughtfully, and if we aren't prepared for the cost we can't be a disciple. The question is: what does this look like in practice?

For us, it means taking Jesus seriously when he said discipleship will have a cost. Have we thought about the effect it might have on our friendships? Or the sinful pleasures we need to kill? Discipleship might mean keeping much less of our money for ourselves. Discipleship may mean we need to change our sexual behaviour; are we prepared to do that? Or is that an intrusion too far?

These are very real costs. It's tempting to dismiss them as secondary but Jesus says to *consider* them. With *consideration* we won't be taken by surprise when issues come up. And we won't fail and be mocked like the builder.

Nothing can take priority over your relationship with your teacher Jesus. Anything that would do so needs to go, or take its new rightful place lower down the list. For example, in verse 26, Jesus said, "If anyone comes to me and does not hate[33] his own father and mother and wife and children and brothers and sisters, yes, even his own life, he cannot be my disciple." What Jesus means is that discipleship must be priority number one. You love God first, love your neighbour second. Choose God first; everything else comes after, which *specifically includes* your family.

For a disciple this means when you reach a conflict between Jesus and the priorities of your family, you need to resolve it in a way that honours God first, rather than compromising on Jesus' teaching to keep your spouse, children or parents happy. This means to *choose* God and *not choose* your family. This is the challenge Jesus sets us.

We know that Jesus loves us, but we are tempted to add, "So Jesus doesn't need me to change anything about myself…" The problem is this isn't true, and this parable is a correction to that. Jesus confronts us with the need to make real changes. Jesus confronts us with the high cost of discipleship.

For us, just like the people Jesus told first, these stories lead to two possible responses. We might conclude the cost is going to be too great and choose not to be a disciple. If that's you, I urge you to consider again what's on offer, the value of the Kingdom of God.

The alternative is to accept that the cost is high but, having faith, grasp it tightly knowing whatever it costs will be worth paying.

---

[33] In the Bible this *hate* can mean to *not choose* or to *pass over*, rather than the *intense loathing* we might first imagine.

Questions for reflection:

What are the dangers of starting something off without thinking it through first?

You could call this attitude "intentional discipleship". It requires thinking and planning. What would "unintentional discipleship" look like, and have you ever seen it?

What does it mean to renounce everything?

One thing you can do

Discuss with someone what the most expensive thing you've ever done was, and whether it was worth it. Compare this to the cost/benefit analysis of being a Christian...

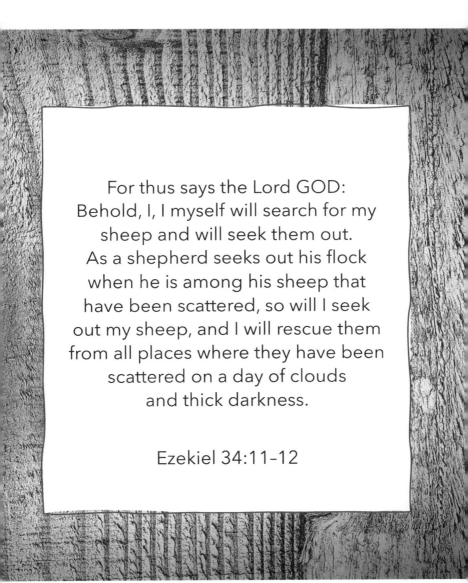

For thus says the Lord GOD: Behold, I, I myself will search for my sheep and will seek them out. As a shepherd seeks out his flock when he is among his sheep that have been scattered, so will I seek out my sheep, and I will rescue them from all places where they have been scattered on a day of clouds and thick darkness.

Ezekiel 34:11-12

14 Finding the Lost

The Lost Sheep and the Lost Coin

Luke 15:4–10

What man of you, having a hundred sheep, if he has lost one of them, does not leave the ninety-nine in the open country, and go after the one that is lost, until he finds it? And when he has found it, he lays it on his shoulder, rejoicing. And when he comes home, he calls together his friends and neighbours, saying to them, "Rejoice with me, for I have found my sheep that was lost." Just so, I tell you, there will be more joy in heaven over one sinner who repents that over ninety-nine righteous persons who need no repentance.

Or what woman, having ten silver coins, if she loses one coin, does not light a lamp and sweep the house and seek diligently until she finds it? And when she has found it, she calls together her friends and neighbours, saying, "Rejoice with me, for I have found the coin that I had lost." Just so, I tell you, there is joy before the angels of God over one sinner who repents."

On our church weekend away once we had the London church planter Richard Coekin join us as a visiting speaker. I remember he suggested we'd know we were finally reaching the whole town when we needed to run special services with cigarette breaks. Somewhere, deep in my Anglican heart, I was more than a little bit horrified. I suspect this was exactly the reaction Richard was hoping for – and I suspect it's very similar to the kind of attitude Jesus was confronting when he told these parables.

In Luke, Chapter 15, we find some parables Jesus addressed to the Pharisees and Scribes: first-century Jewish religious officials. Jesus needed to confront a bad attitude they had, which was revealed by their anger at Jesus spending so much time with people who, in their view, weren't the right sort of company. The Pharisees, for instance, absolutely hated the Jewish tax collectors who'd sold out to the Romans and lived off a cut of what they collected. And they were completely revolted by "sinners", men and women who lived shameful lives.[34] The Pharisees grumbled about Jesus' reaching out to these people. They felt it was incompatible with being a godly teacher or a prophet. They didn't understand: how could someone sent from God spend time with people like these?

Over the course of three short stories, Jesus blows apart their thinking and explains why his behaviour is not only compatible, but sits at the very heart of why he came. The three stories are known as the Parable of the Lost Sheep, the Parable of the Lost Coin and the Parable of the Prodigal Son. In this chapter we will look at the sheep and the coin together.

We begin with the sheep. I realise there is a fair chance you've never been left in charge of sheep, in which case you'll need to trust me when I tell you they can't always look after themselves very well. They try to stick together, which is the only defence they have. On

---

[34] Many of whom worked in what we'd call the "adult" industries.

their own they are vulnerable. During the day the flock spreads out to graze and the hapless ones can get separated. Sometimes it's because they get spooked and run off; sometimes curiosity gets the better of them and they wander from the flock; sometimes they're just daft and get their fleece tangled in bushes or fence wire, or they fall into water and can't climb out. There are so many ways sheep can get into trouble.

If any of you lost a sheep, Jesus implies, you'd go off looking for it, even if that meant leaving ninety-nine other sheep on their own in the field. A good shepherd, rather than just accepting his loss, will go and search for the missing one. Then, Jesus continues, once he finds it, given that it's too exhausted to walk, he'll carry it home himself and return it to the flock. The shepherd will do this for *one* in *one hundred*.

Jesus follows up with the parable of the lost coin. Luke often recorded Jesus using men and women in corresponding stories and here's an example.[35] Whereas the shepherd was a man, Jesus now tells us about a woman in a household who has lost a valuable silver coin, probably a day's wage – quite possibly part of her dowry. Rather than giving it up as lost, she lights a lamp and sweeps the house top to bottom until she finds it. This is a diligent search

---

[35] The shepherd would be a rough and rugged cowboy-type figure, with a strong smell of the countryside and generally not considered good company by the higher classes like the Pharisees and the Scribes – who would also have looked down on the woman. Both the examples Jesus uses are from the lower rungs of society.

involving time, effort and investment.[36] She does this, even though she has another nine coins that never got lost.

As I write this, I realise that coins and sheep have similarities. Both are easily lost, both are valuable to the owner and both are at risk from predators and thieves.

Jesus' point to the religious authorities is simple. Neither the safe sheep in the field nor the coins tucked in the purse are what the owner needs to worry about.

If it's true about shepherds and women, with their lost sheep and coins, how much truer with our loving father God, looking over his people? His heart is moved for the lost. Those who have wandered to the enemy, or are entangled in sinful habits, or drowning in their circumstances. Motivated by compassion, Jesus seeks them out. Jesus is *missional* about going out to the sinners, rather than hanging around with the saints. Jesus came to bring change, not join a club for the holy – much to the annoyance of the Pharisees.

Let's look at how these stories end: celebration! The shepherd and the woman are both so overjoyed to find their sheep and coin that they run out to find their friends and neighbours. Now, it's always a relief when you find something, but in these little stories the celebration is so *big* it feels out of place. Why? Because we're being pointed towards the spiritual message of this pair of parables, God's *delight* at sinners who repent and turn back to him.

Jesus teaches us it is a joyful day in Heaven when one of these people turns away from their sinful lives to be carried back to safety. There

---

[36] Lamp oil and wick weren't free.

is more joy over one of these people[37] than over ninety-nine who don't believe they are lost.

Jesus' mission to the lost is deeply embedded in these explosive parables, but the lesson you take home will depend on how you see yourself.

Are you feeling like the Pharisees, finding the sight of Jesus running after sinners a bit disappointing? Perhaps you've worked hard at your own purity, so now, feeling worthy, want to stand in the company of Jesus – *without* mixing with the impure? Are you attractive to Jesus in a way that other people are not? Is your church too good for the newcomer you've seen drinking in the pub? What about the new family who struggle to control their children... do we really need to have *their sort* in here?

This kind of thinking is the error of the Pharisees. Jesus warned them and *he warns us* too.

On the other hand, if you believe Jesus, and know you are redeemed – know that your sins have been paid for by his perfect sacrifice – you can watch happily while your good shepherd looks for others to bring home.

Or, if you realise you are lost, be thankful Jesus wants to find you. Now, rest on his shoulders and be carried back into his flock, knowing, incredibly, you have been the cause of great *joy in Heaven*.

---

[37] People who the Pharisees think are too dirty to talk to.

Questions for reflection:

How do you naturally respond when new people join your church? Especially new people who don't quite "fit" into your idea of Jesus' church?

Does Jesus' mission to the lost inspire you or confront you, or is it a bit of both?

How might we need to challenge our thinking if we have developed a little of the Pharisee-ish tendency?

Are you ready to join in the celebrations in Heaven when one of these sinners repents?

One thing you can do

If you're part of a church, today is a good day to put forward a new idea that would make a church "misfit" feel more welcome. Could that be a smoking shelter, or better childcare for new families, or a new meeting at a different time of day?

OR – If you aren't a church member, go to one, whether you feel like you "fit" or not!

---

15 The Repentant Are Welcome

The Prodigal (Wasteful) Son

Luke 15:11–32

And he said, "There was a man who had two sons. And the younger of them said to his father, 'Father, give me the share of property that is coming to me.' And he divided his property between them. Not many days later, the younger son gathered all he had and took a journey into a far country, and there he squandered his property in reckless living. And when he had spent everything, a severe famine arose in that country, and he began to be in need. So he went and hired himself out to one of the citizens of that country, who sent him into his fields to feed pigs. And he was longing to be fed with the pods that the pigs ate, and no one gave him anything. But when he came to himself, he said, 'How many of my father's hired servants have more than enough bread, but I perish here in hunger! I will arise and go to my father, and I will say to him, "Father, I have sinned against heaven and before you. I am no longer worthy to be called your son. Treat me as one of your hired servants."' And he arose and came to his father. But while he was still a long way off, his father saw him and felt compassion, and ran and embraced him and kissed him. And the son said to him, 'Father I have sinned against heaven and before you. I am no longer worthy to be called your son.' But the father said to his servants, 'Bring quickly the best robe, and put it on him, and put a ring on his finger, and shoes on his feet. And bring the fatted calf and kill it, let us eat and celebrate. For this my son was dead, and is alive again; he was lost and is found.' And they began to celebrate. Now his older son was in the field, and as he came and drew near to the house, he heard music and dancing. And he called one of the servants and asked what these things meant. And he said to him, 'Your brother has come, and your father has killed the fattened calf, because he has received him back safe and sound.' But he was angry and refused to go in. His father came out and entreated him, but he answered his father, 'Look, these many years I have served you, and I never disobeyed your command, yet you never gave me a young goat, that I might celebrate with my friends. But when this son of yours came, who has devoured your property with prostitutes, you killed the fattened calf for him!' And he said to him, 'Son, you are always with me, and all that is mine is yours. It was fitting to celebrate and be glad, for this your brother was dead, and is alive; he was lost and is found.'"

You can tell *anyone* your bad news. Have you ever noticed the number of viral news stories are about people's *bad news* — like lottery winners who hit hard times? Do you wonder why we love to read about that sort of thing? Apparently you can tell who your real friends are because they enjoy hearing your *good news*. I heard the popular Canadian psychologist Jordan Peterson say that, and I think there's a lot of truth in it – and also an insight into the begrudging tendency of the older brother in this parable.

Jesus told this story to the Pharisees, as the finale of a triple-parable teaching session about finding the lost. Moving in his sequence from sheep to coins, to brothers, Jesus crystallised his teaching. First there was a lost sheep, one of a hundred, whom the shepherd seeks and finds. Then there was a lost coin, one of ten, which leads the woman to search the whole house over. We considered both of these in the previous chapter.

Now in this much longer story we have a son, one of two, who takes his whole inheritance early, runs off, squanders it all, hits rock bottom… and returns. Their father restores him into the family *and* throws a party – much to the annoyance of his older brother. Although the story seems to follow the younger brother, the focus of the parable is actually the reaction of the older brother, because it's *his* attitude that Jesus uses to challenge the Pharisees.

The Pharisees will have known the father represents God, and the older brother represents those who have stuck to the rules all their life and "never disobeyed" the commands of God… people like the Pharisees. The younger son, the prodigal,[38] is representing sinners. The kind of lost person that Jesus is reaching out to.

---

[38] Prodigal means wasteful.

In the story the younger son grabs whatever he can and he runs far off, away from the watchful eyes of his father. He wastes his father's money on the filthiest lifestyle until he has nothing left. Eventually he's trying to make a living tending pigs in gentile lands. He's got so hungry he finds himself daydreaming about sharing meals with the pigs – animals that Jews wouldn't normally be near. We can imagine him chewing on their muddy bean pods to stave off hunger. There isn't any further to fall.

But... *he awakes*: his eyes are opened to the life he left behind. He remembers the blessings that even his father's workers have, and decides he'd rather go back as a servant to his family than stay in the mess where he is. Then *he repents*: he "turns around" and goes back, to where his father has been waiting. Then *he is restored*: the father immediately restores him, dressing him in the best robe and replacing his shoes and his ring – a symbol of family membership.

When the older son gets back from work and sees this, he is upset. He won't go inside; he cannot even call this man his brother anymore. It falls to their father to try to reconcile them. "Your brother" – he reminds him they are brothers – "was dead and is alive!"

Those who have served God dutifully many years should be absolutely *delighted* when the lost awake, repent and are restored. But too often that isn't our honest reaction. We can be quick to object to their good fortune, treating them like the resented lottery winners in news articles – perhaps hoping for a downfall. Jesus first spoke this parable to the Pharisees, who'd have identified themselves with the older brother. I suspect most evangelical Christians reading it today would be a little too quick to see the Pharisees being condemned, without noticing they have one leg in the same trap. Forgetting the generosity shown us, we get offended by God showing grace to someone else. Because of our time served, or the orthodoxy of our church, or because we are so sure we have everything right, we can feel like we're a better grade than the new convert. We can try to *show them up*, when we should be *showing them the way*.

We must remember we have all been like the younger brother once. At some point we "came to ourselves" and underwent a conversion like him. God received us gladly, like the father in the parable did, and welcomed us in. Perhaps if we remember this, we might not resent the generosity of God.

Reading Luke, Chapter 15, is hearing Jesus' mission to the lost, in his own words. It's never more crystallised than in this conversion story about a son. A wasteful, wandering squanderer – who repents and is restored – but finds himself rejected by the "righteous".

Questions for reflection:

Have you ever caught yourself thinking like the older brother?

Do you remember being the younger brother? Sharing your story of when you "came to yourself" and returned to God is a great way to remain thankful and avoid the trap of becoming resentful.

One thing you can do

Write your testimony out thinking about the little details; like how God spoke to you through the Bible, through people, and events, until you "came to yourself" and embraced your heavenly father.

When it's ready, share it with someone.

16 Growing among Weeds

The Wheat and the Tares

Matthew 13:24-30 (explained vv36-43)

He put another parable before them, saying, "The kingdom of Heaven may be compared to a man who sowed good seed in his field, but while his men were sleeping, his enemy came and sowed weeds among the wheat and went away. So when the plants came up and bore grain, then the weeds appeared also. And the servants of the master of the house came and said to him, 'Master, did you not sow good seed in your field? How then does it have weeds?' He said to them, 'An enemy has done this.' So the servants said to him, 'Then do you want us to go and gather them?' But he said, 'No, lest in gathering the weeds you root up the wheat along with them. Let both grow together until the harvest, and at harvest time I will tell the reapers, "Gather the weeds first and bind them in bundles to be burned, but gather the wheat into my barn."'"

Our garden is on the edge of fields. The farmer leaves a narrow strip of land untended, where the big tractors can't easily reach, so here every kind of weed grows and releases their seeds into the wind – to land in my vegetable beds. If we go on holiday, when I come back huge thistles and weeds will have grown in between our carrots and onions. They can get so big that pulling them out does more damage than leaving them in.

In the Gospel of Matthew, Chapter 13, Jesus uses parables to teach us about the world we live in, and the spiritual realities behind it. This is also one of many agricultural parables... While the Parable of the Sower (Chapter 2) taught us that different listeners respond differently to God's word, this (equally agricultural) parable teaches us about living around weeds. Perhaps we need to begin by being clear about what weeds are. In the Parable of the Sower the weeds were symbols for *worldly distractions*, that is, things that choke out the Word and prevent disciples growing strong. Now, in the Parable of the Wheat and the Tares, the *weeds* are the "sons of the evil one" planted by the devil; these *weeds* are *worldly people*. So, even though we have similar images, the weeds are something different and the emphasis of the teaching is different.

In the world, therefore, we will expect to mix with both the wheat and the weeds. Wheaty, fruitful people mix with weedy, fruitless, worldly people.

One implication of this is that people will disappoint us. We will be rustling leaves with people quite different to us. Among these there will be people we're close to who, spiritually speaking, couldn't be more opposed to us.

And we won't be able to avoid it, because the wheat and the weeds are in the same places. Whether that means your high street, your school, your workplace or your church, wherever you meet people you will find both wheat and weeds. We might be tempted to draw a line around everyone in church on a Sunday and label them "going to Heaven", and then draw another line around everyone in the betting shop on a Sunday and label these people "going to Hell". But we haven't been put in a neatly segregated world.[39] As a result it's quite likely that some of your best friends are weeds known only to God, and equally likely you'll be in Heaven for eternity with the kind of people you'd avoid sitting next to on a train. There's something to think about…

Which brings me to something else I learned from growing vegetables, which is, especially in the early stages, it's not always easy to identify which plants are the seeds you planted and which are the weeds. The more mature the plants grow, the more obvious the difference. It takes time before a carrot plant has an edible orange root. On a thistle it takes time before the thorns appear. People are the same: they either get fruitier or pricklier with age. That feels like a good enough reason not to try to sweep in before God, pretending to be the judge. (If you needed a reason.)

Nevertheless, the end of the story is this: the weeds *are* gathered up, tied into bundles and burned. The wheat is collected as well, but it's taken into the barn of the owner. The two kinds of plant couldn't have more different ends. Although they were allowed to grow together to maturity, a time came when they were separated and sent to very different places.

Harvest is when this happens, which is Bible language for the wrapping up of all time: the end. At harvest the wheat and weeds show themselves. The wheat has produced a good crop but the weed has just been a hindrance all along. Sucking up the goodness of the

---

[39] Even the garden of Eden had a snake in it.

soil without offering up a return on it. A thorn in the side of the wheat, so to speak. It turns out that the only reason the weeds were allowed to stay in the soil was so the wheat wouldn't get damaged by pulling them out.

We will mix with weeds and wheat; we won't know who is which but we will grow alongside each other, sharing our churches, trains, workspaces and even homes. This means at times our human relationships will cause pain and conflict. For now we must *bear with* each other, loving and encouraging each other however hard that may be. Then eventually some of us will *bear fruit* and others will not.

All people are known to God, who, alone, is the final judge. (Not us!) Eventually his justice will arrive in the form of a great sorting. And, when this time comes, all the wheat will be gathered up, weed-free, into the Lord's eternal barn.

Questions for reflection:

We can sometimes think of our churches as though they are like Heaven, weed-free, basically just a refuge for the saved. But have you seen evidence that they are not?

Can you think of a time when it benefitted you to face a challenge caused by "growing next to a weed"?

Would it help you if God told you who is wheat and who is a weed?

Are you thankful to God for delaying his harvest?

One thing you can do

Next time you meet a stranger, keep in mind that God has *deliberately* left both wheat and weeds together on the earth, and this person you are speaking to might well be someone you will spend the rest of eternity with.

"Not-a-Parables" of the Rolex and Aston Martin

A young woman was rummaging through boxes at an auction and came across a case of old costume jewellery and watches. Most of it was corroded and broken but mixed in with the junk she found a valuable old Rolex. Quickly, pushing it to the bottom, she hid it again. Trying to disguise her happiness, she ran out of the auction and sold everything she had to buy that box.

A collector of cars had amassed a very fine assortment of vehicles, of all ages and types, although he had a particular fondness for vintage British sports cars. This is understandable because they are very nice. He was most pleased with them and stored them carefully in his big garage block on a country estate. Nevertheless, when he discovered a pristine Aston Martin DB4A, he ran to sell every one of them so that he could acquire this very unusual vehicle. Even though his garage was now empty his new car was a source of great joy.

17 The Valuable Kingdom

The Hidden Treasure and Pearl of Great Value

Matthew 13:44-46

The kingdom of heaven is like treasure hidden in a field, which a man found and covered up. Then in his joy he goes and sells all that he has and buys that field.

Again, the Kingdom of Heaven is like a merchant in search of fine pearls, who, on finding one pearl of great value, went and sold all that he had and bought it.

Question: what do you make sacrifices for? Or: what does it take for you to give something up? As an example, sometimes I might forgo a sticky bun for the benefit of my health; we could say I've made a small sacrifice to look after my own body. Perhaps you'd pay for music lessons for your daughter. That's a financial sacrifice for your child. Do you do the washing-up after eating your evening meal? That is a sacrifice of time now, for the benefit of an enjoyable breakfast in the morning without last night's dishes casting judgement on you from the sink.

So we are all giving things up, all the time! Perhaps you hadn't already realised that. The question we usually ask when we are thinking about a sacrifice is: will it be worth it?

For instance, even though I love eating sticky buns, it isn't good to be overweight – and that's definitely a risk living in the UK with so many delicious bun shops around – therefore it's worth me controlling my calories. And, even though it's expensive, the experience of learning music will be valuable to my child; therefore I will sacrifice some of my earnings to pay for this. (Luckily I just saved some money by walking past the bakery.) Or, even though I'd prefer to go to bed, I don't enjoy my coffee in the morning when the sink is full of dishes; therefore I will wash them now.

In Matthew, Chapter 13, Jesus uses parables to teach about the nature of the kingdom. We have already considered the Parables of the Sower, the Wheat and the Tares[40] and the Mustard Seed. All of them begin with "The Kingdom of Heaven[41] *is like...*" so we know each of these parables is included purposely to tell us what the kingdom *is like*. So, now, what do these two new short stories about valuable things add to our knowledge of the Kingdom of Heaven?

In the first, a man discovers a hidden stash of treasure on a patch of ground he didn't own. Was this unusual? Perhaps, but valuables in those days were things like gold and silver, which are harder to transfer than BACS payments, and this predates Bitcoin. Hiding them in the ground,[42] with the intention of returning to recover them, was a common form of security. With the turbulent history of war, rising and falling empires, exile and return, we can imagine they got lost from time to time. Perhaps the original owner was killed in war, or exiled and unable to return. Or perhaps the family returned

---

[40] Or Weeds

[41] Well, apart from the Sower, which Jesus explains is about "hearing the Word of the Kingdom" so it's slightly different in emphasis.

[42] Away from prying eyes, but in a place you'll remember.

but were never able to find the spot grandad said he left the stash of gold.

Whatever the story behind it, the man finds treasure hidden in this field. What he does next is cover it back up, because it's not his and nobody else knows it's there. Then he goes and sells absolutely everything he owns to buy that field so he can collect the stash. Whether that's morally dubious[43] or not isn't the main point, Jesus doesn't pass comment. The focus is that this man knew the *field had value*, others didn't, and crucially he is prepared to give up everything else he had *to get ownership of it.*

Likewise, the pearl merchant, finding a very special pearl[44] that has caught his eye – for its exceptional size and beauty, we imagine – goes and sells everything he owns to purchase this one pearl. Is that good business sense? Jesus, again, doesn't pass comment. But it's bizarre: the man is now presumably homeless, and encumbered with a massive pearl. The point is that this experienced pearl merchant *knew his pearls*, and he'd recognised great value in this particular one. Like the man in the field, he was prepared to give up everything he had *to acquire the thing he wanted.*

Jesus says the Kingdom of Heaven is like this. When you recognise the value of it, you'll understand that it is better than everything else you ever wanted. The Kingdom of Heaven is worth more than

---

[43] If he'd wanted to be more dubious he could have just stolen it without buying the field...
[44] Pearls were enormously valuable in the day – they couldn't be faked, and diving for them was dangerous.

anything else you have ever owned, can own, or even imagine owning.

If your health is worth skipping a sticky bun for, the Kingdom of God is worth starving to death for, if that were what it cost. If music lessons are worth a few pounds of your hard-earned cash, the Kingdom of God is worth all of it, and your pension too if need be. If your relaxed breakfast is worth doing the dishes in the evening, the Kingdom of God is worth doing everyone's dishes forever, if that were what it took. Jesus wants us to know that it's ridiculous to place a higher value on anything else. If we do, then we haven't fully understood its worth.

Both the man with the treasure and the pearl merchant understood their "field". Treasure man understood what was in his literal field, and pearl man was an expert in his "field". The "field" we need to be an expert in is the Kingdom of Heaven, and if we understand it properly we won't be letting other stuff get in the way. We will be ready give up everything to take possession of it.

Questions for reflection:

What sacrifices do you make for the Kingdom of Heaven?

Or what are you prepared to give up to gain the Kingdom of Heaven?

What are you not prepared to give up? Maybe that's where we need to finish…

One thing you can do

See if you can find something in your home that is better than everlasting life with Jesus.

The point is that you can't; but it's a useful exercise for keeping things in perspective.

---

18 The Great Divide

The Net

Matthew 13:47-50

Again, the Kingdom of Heaven is like a net that was thrown into the sea and gathered fish of every kind. When it was full, men drew it ashore and sat down and sorted the good into containers but threw away the bad. So it will be at the end of the age. The angels will come out and separate the evil from the righteous and throw them into the fiery furnace. In that place there will be weeping and gnashing of teeth.

Like the modern practice of trawler fishing, although on a much smaller and less destructive scale, drag nets were used in Jesus' time to catch fish from the side of a boat. Stones with holes drilled in them were used as weights at the bottom, and cork floats at the top, caused the net to open wide when you threw it into the sea. The fishermen could then haul the net in to land their fish. Net fishing was hard work – it was also very familiar work for Jesus' listeners around Capernaum – several of his disciples knew the trade very well since it was the family business.

These disciples would have also known that fishing with a net was indiscriminate. When you fish with a net you scoop up whatever is there, not just saleable fish, called the *catch*, but also what fishermen call the *bycatch*. In the story Jesus told, he said this net gathered fish "of every kind", i.e. there was no kind of fish that this net didn't gather. The Kingdom of Heaven *is like that*, we are told.

We are then told that the Kingdom of Heaven, having gathered all kinds of fish, *is like* the net brought ashore, and sorted through. These fish of all kinds are divided into only two groups. The good and the bad. This means that, at the end of the age, the world, which currently contains all different kinds of people, will be divided into only two kinds. The righteous kind and the evil kind.

What do we take away from this story? Coming shortly after the Parable of the Wheat and the Tares, Jesus is continuing his teaching about the end of time. Although the theme is similar, there are differences between these two parables. Whereas before the wheat and the weeds were growing together, now the good and bad are swimming together.[45] The wheat and the weeds were allowed to grow together for the benefit of the wheat, but there is no mention here of a reason the fish were left mixed together in the sea. Instead, in this parable, the whole emphasis is on the *sorting*.

Another difference is that the wheat and weeds were only two kinds to begin with. In the net there are "fish of every kind". To an audience in the Roman empire, a cultural melting pot, this (explosively) meant the inclusion of other non-Jewish (gentile) races. Even though scripture has always hinted at this from the beginning, it was still uncomfortable to hear. In fact, the Jewish religious authorities had been encouraging their cultural distinctiveness, which hadn't faded under Roman occupation. The call to be God's blessing for *the nations* had slipped onto the backburner; it turns out running

---

[45] Or they had been, but now they are caught in the same net.

an exclusive cult in the temple was much less *complicated* than being a light on the hill.

Reading a parable like this one today in our globalised world might not seem as radical as it would have in the first century. However, I encourage us to be challenged. At the very least, we should recognise that Christians won't all look and sound the same as us. Most of us worship in churches that have a lot of social, economic, cultural and racial similarity, and there might not be much you can do about it if your church represents the surrounding area. But do think about it honestly: your local church should be a mixture of all the local fish otherwise it's not reflecting what the Kingdom of God is like. Big fish, immigrant fish, little fish, rich fish, new fish, old fish, poor fish, black fish, young fish, white fish...

However you categorise your fish, the ending of the story Jesus told is where the main emphasis lies. The final end-time sorting, from all the kinds in the net, into two categories, *catch* and *bycatch* – righteous and evil.

Likewise, wherever you were swimming, whoever you were with, whatever your size, race, wealth, age or health... whatever. The only thing that will matter when the sorting time arrives is your membership of one of these; righteous or evil.

Righteous, meaning right with God, or evil, meaning opposed to God.

To be right with God, and therefore saved, you must accept as a gift the righteousness of Jesus. Then, when the sorter looks at you in the net, they will not see evil but, instead, glinting in the sun, the spotless righteousness of Jesus.

It was earned by Jesus, at great cost, by his sinless life and sacrificial death, and transferred to you, by faith, for free.

Questions for reflection:

What does a Christian look like?

Consider your local church. How well does it reflect your local area? Are any fish missing?

Knowing that there is a great sorting coming, how should that change our daily priorities in the meantime?

One thing you can do

The ultimate final sorting will be between the "evil" and the "righteous". For or against Jesus. The righteous will come from across all the groups we might normally sort people into.

Choose a group of people local to you, whom you don't know much about and who aren't well represented in the local Christian community. Aim to get to know them better – you might hang out where they hang out – or start a new hobby – follow a new sport – join a club…

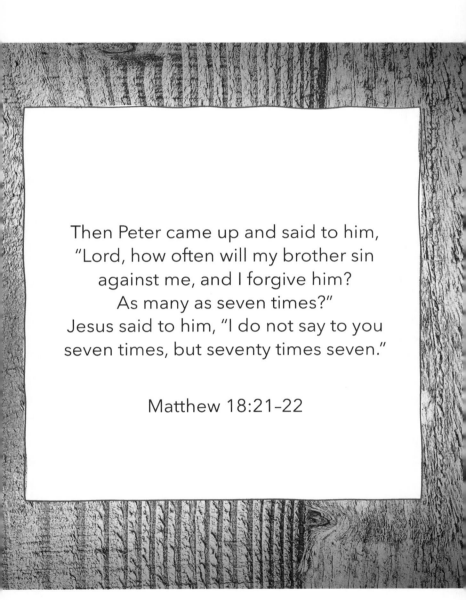

Then Peter came up and said to him,
"Lord, how often will my brother sin
against me, and I forgive him?
As many as seven times?"
Jesus said to him, "I do not say to you
seven times, but seventy times seven."

Matthew 18:21–22

19 Forgiveness: The Rule

The Unforgiving Servant

Matthew 18:23-35

Therefore the kingdom of heaven may be compared to a king who wished to settle accounts with his servants. When he began to settle, one was brought to him who owed him ten thousand talents. And since he could not pay, his master ordered him to be sold, with his wife and children and all that he had, and payment to be made. So the servant fell on his knees, imploring him, "Have patience with me, and I will pay you everything." And out of pity for him, the master of that servant released him and forgave him the debt. But when that same servant went out, he found one of his fellow servants who owed him a hundred denarii, and seizing him, he began to choke him, saying, "Pay what you owe." So his fellow servant fell down and pleaded with him, "Have patience with me, and I will pay you." He refused and went and put him in prison until he should pay the debt. When his fellow servants saw what had taken place, they were greatly distressed, and they went and reported to their master all that had taken place. Then his master summoned him and said to him, "You wicked servant! I forgave you all that debt because you pleaded with me. And should not you have had mercy on your fellow servant, as I had mercy on you?" And in anger his master delivered him to the jailers, until he should pay all his debt. So also my heavenly Father will do to every one of you, if you do not forgive your brother from your heart.

Jesus told this parable to Peter, and the other disciples, as part of his teaching on forgiveness *among brothers*, or, in other words, fellow believers. After Jesus gave his instructions for reconciliation[46] following sin against you by another Christian, Peter wants to know *how many times* he should be expected to forgive. The Pharisees traditionally said three chances was enough, then give up. Peter goes further, and suggests seven times. But "loads of times" is Jesus' answer.[47] Whatever it takes.

The parable tells us about a king settling accounts with his servants. Some of them have racked up *inconceivably* large debts. The debt of the one who can't pay is ten thousand talents, which – for context – was several times over what Herod collected in taxes each year. It's like when a child makes up a number "You owe me a million trillion billion million thousand pounds!" The servant can't ever hope to pay it, which is the main point.

The king's order was exactly what everyone expected. If he can't pay, take it away. But not just his land and possessions, also his wife and

---

[46] Or not reconciliation, depending on repentance.

[47] *Literally* he said either seventy-seven, or seventy times seven (depending on how you translate it) but almost certainly, given that seven was the number symbolising perfection and completion, what he meant was "however many times it takes!"

children. Divide them up, sell them off. The king plans to take *everything* against the debt. It might sound horrible to us, and it was, but at the time it was really just standard procedure. Jesus wasn't intending to shock the audience with that bit.

However, when the servant pleads his case (brace yourself: here comes the bomb), the king relents and lets him off. Wow! The other servants must have been amazed. But what happens next enrages them. It turns out that the forgiven servant also had money owed *to him* by another servant. A tiny amount in comparison. This was like lunch money. And what he does is seek out this man and *violently* demand payment from him. When the man can't pay, he drags him to court and has him jailed.

Well, this terrible injustice is reported back to the king, and the king is mad about it. He comes down hard on the unforgiving servant and throws him in jail.

Jesus says the Kingdom of Heaven can *be compared to* this.

The lesson of the story is we must always remember how generously God has forgiven us. Having been forgiven for so much, we need to be mindful how we treat others who sin against us. We have had our slates wiped clean but that doesn't mean we deserved it, or did it ourselves. Like a million-trillion-pound debt we could never afford – we were beyond helping ourselves.

God has established a kingdom of unbelievable grace. The kind of grace that makes you say wow! Having been accepted into this kingdom, we show we can accept his rules by following his example. We might object; we might protest that we don't want to be like a doormat, with people walking all over us. But if we don't forgive we are being hypocrites, and rejecting the kingdom of grace. In turn we will be rejected by God, and removed from his kingdom.

When Peter asked what the *limits* were on forgiveness it showed he hadn't quite grasped how this kingdom works yet. When we're asked to forgive our Christian brothers and sisters *as many times as it takes*, we are being taught to reflect some of the grace that Jesus has shown to us.

Questions for reflection:

Refusing to forgive a repentant sinner isn't our right; it's a hypocrisy. But how quickly should we forgive?

Matthew 18:15–20 includes a reminder that when two or three gather in his name, he is with us. In what circumstances are these people gathered?

What happens if we fail to forgive our "brothers" who sin against us?

One thing you can do

Forgiving someone is an action, a thing we choose to do (rather than something we wait for our hearts to *feel*). If there is something you should have forgiven but instead have resolved not to - start to correct that today. Ask for God's help.

"Not-a-Parable" of the Birthday

A little girl was looking forward to her birthday. She had been involved in the planning all week. She had shared her love for a particular toy that she had seen in a cartoon show, *Little Hairy Pony*. This little pink thing with a brushable mane had well and truly stolen her heart. She wanted nothing more.

So the party was themed by *Little Hairy Pony*. The cake was *Little Hairy Pony*. The decorations were *Little Hairy Pony*. Everything was, and what she was looking forward to most was her present. She had asked for a "Little Hairy Pony Strawberry Scented Deluxe Playset, with Stable"!

When present time came, her mother first said she had favours for all the girls at the party! So the first girl was handed a big box, and she unwrapped… a "Little Hairy Pony Strawberry Scented Deluxe Playset, with Stable." Wow! The next girl, too, is handed a box, and it was another "Little Hairy Pony Strawberry Scented Deluxe Playset"! And another and so on, until they each had a playset.

The birthday girl was excited. If this is the size of the party favours, what will she receive? Maybe a real-life living pony…

The birthday girl is handed a colourful present. She unwraps it. To her massive disappointment, it's exactly what she asked for, a "Little Hairy Pony Strawberry Scented Deluxe Playset, with Stable."

"What's this?" she asks, starting to become upset. "It's my birthday and you've given me exactly the same present as everyone else!"

"I'm sorry," says her mother, "I thought it would be nice to be generous. Can't I do that? I thought you would be happy for your friends."

20 A Generous God

The Labourers in The Vineyard

Matthew 20:1-16

For the kingdom of heaven is like a master of a house who went out early in the morning to hire labourers for his vineyard. After agreeing with the labourers for a denarius a day, he sent them into his vineyard. And going out about the third hour he saw others standing idle in the market-place, and to them he said, "You go into the vineyard too, and whatever is right I will give you." So they went. Going out again about the sixth hour and the ninth hour, he did the same. And about the eleventh hour he went out and found others standing. And he said to them, "Why do you stand here idle all day?" They said to him, "Because no one has hired us." He said to them, "You go into the vineyard too." And when evening came, the owner of the vineyard said to his foreman, "Call the labourers and pay them their wages, beginning with the last, up to the first." And when those hired about the eleventh hour came, each of them received a denarius. Now when those hired first came, they thought they would receive more, but each of them also received a denarius. And on receiving it they grumbled at the master of the house, saying, "These last worked only one hour, and you have made them equal to us who have borne the burden of the day and the scorching heat." But he replied to one of them, "Friend, I am doing you no wrong. Did you not agree with me for a denarius? Take what belongs to you and go. I choose to give to this last worker as I give to you. Am I not allowed to do what I choose with what belongs to me? Or do you begrudge my generosity?" So the last will be first, and the first last.

D id you have a sibling as a child? If you did, how much did you enjoy watching them open their birthday presents when you didn't have any of your own?

Or have you ever applied for a job you really wanted and missed out? How did you feel about the happy person who took your place? It's all too easy to begrudge generosity.[48]

Jesus began this parable by saying "For the Kingdom of Heaven is like [this]." Because Jesus is telling us that the Kingdom of Heaven is like this story of a vineyard owner. And because he ended it on a *sharp correction* of the disappointed labourers who begrudge his generosity, this was his main point. The parable is about the *generosity* of God, and a warning *not to be begrudging about it.*

Matthew included this parable shortly after the Unforgiving Servant, as part of a block of teaching about living in the new kingdom (Matthew 18–20). Many topics are covered: an attitude to forgiveness, the sanctity of marriage, the welcome of children, and loosening our hold on wealth. Then Peter, with his customary

---

[48] Except, of course, when it's offered to us.

bluntness, asked what their[49] reward will be for all this hard work. Jesus began by telling them that the rewards will be great, a hundredfold, and eternal life – in other words, much greater than you can imagine and far more than you could ever manage to give up. Then he offered this parable to give us more of an answer.

The Kingdom of Heaven is God's kingdom with God's rules. For those who are citizens there are fantastic benefits. None of the labourers went unpaid. The early labourers were treated completely fairly. A denarius was a full day's wage. It's what they happily agreed to. They chose it: a fair pay for a fair day's work. They weren't kept waiting for pay, nor were they cheated with deductions or unexpected uniform cleaning fees... etc... This is all happening in a culture where paid work was uncertain, and the poor had little protection from unfair practices, or support if employment wasn't available. In principle, they were happy men; this was a *good* day for them.

Then, during the day the owner returned to the marketplace several more times, and each time he collected up more workers to finish the job.[50] These workers had sat waiting in the marketplace, some for hours, some for half of the day, some for practically the whole day, and must have been about to give up and go home. But when hired they must have been happy: some work and some pay is better than no work and no pay.

---

[49] Meaning the disciples'.
[50] Whatever vineyard job it was, we aren't told, but probably a harvest fits best with this urgency.

Everyone was content until pay time. Then the *grumbling* started. Not for the late arrivals, they'd have been delighted to receive a full day's wage. But when the early workers realised they'd all been paid the same they were annoyed. They begrudged the generosity towards the latecomers.

As with many parables, where your heart is will dictate the character you most naturally identify yourself with. Among the disciples there was likely to be a pecking order forming. Peter and Andrew, who were chosen first, might have identified themselves as early workers, and seen all the others as the late arrivals. Or the twelve might have seen themselves as early workers, and everyone else as late. Or all the men might have seen themselves as truer followers than the women. Or the disciples might have wondered if they were the late ones and the early workers were the temple leaders.

Thinking back to Peter's question to Jesus, about what the disciples' reward will be, his real question to Jesus wasn't "will your followers be rewarded, Jesus?" – to which the plain answer is yes – his question was more like "will we disciples be distinguished and *especially privileged over other followers* for getting in first?" This question reveals a heart issue. Having received the grace of God, we expect to be paid for our loyalty.

The parable is a correction to this attitude, then, a reminder of God's grace, and a warning not to elevate ourselves and then grumble at God's generosity when we see it offered to others. After all, we didn't grumble when it was first offered to us.

There is no pecking order in the Kingdom of Heaven; each are offered the same reward. The first are the same as the last, and the last are the same as the first.

Questions for reflection:

Do you find it easy to watch other people open birthday presents?

How can you keep yourself from the temptation to grumble and resent God's generosity to others?

If the first is the same as the last and there is no ranking in the Kingdom of Heaven, should we delay until the final moment to serve the Master?

One thing you can do

Find another believer and tell them how pleased you are that they share your faith in Jesus, and what a privilege it is to work together for the Kingdom of Heaven.

"Not-a-Parable" of the Dishwasher

My children don't like unloading the dishwasher, even though, as I keep reminding them, they should be thankful because owning a dishwasher is a blessing and so much easier than washing it all by hand. As I headed outside for a moment I asked my two daughters to unload the dishwasher and put the plates away. One said "Sure!" but carried on watching TV. The other one said, "Why! I did it last Wednesday! It's so unfair!" and stomped off into another room.

When I returned, daughter one, who promised to do it, was still watching TV. My other daughter was just putting away the last plate.

So which of my daughters was the obedient one?

"And he will turn many of the children of Israel to the Lord their God, and he will go before him in the spirit and power of Elijah, to turn the hearts of the fathers to the children, and the disobedient to the wisdom of the just, to make ready for the Lord a people prepared."

Luke 1:16-17

(An angel of the Lord, speaking to Zechariah about John the Baptist)

21 Practical Obedience

The Two Sons

Matthew 21:28-32

What do you think? A man had two sons. And he went to the first and said, "Son, go and work in the vineyard today." And he answered, "I will not", but afterwards he changed his mind and went. And he went to the other son and said the same. And he answered, "I go, sir", but did not go. Which of the two did the will of his father?" They said, "The first." Jesus said to them, "Truly, I say to you, the tax collectors and the prostitutes go into the kingdom of God before you. For John came to you in the way of righteousness, and you did not believe him, but the tax collectors and the prostitutes believed him. And even when you saw it, you did not afterwards change your minds and believe him.

On the morning he told this parable, Jesus had been walking to the temple and killed a fig tree with a simple word, just because it didn't have figs on it when he was hungry. This was unusual. The disciples marvelled at it: to them I expect it looked like everything was coming to a head. It was. In fact, everything in Jesus' ministry had been leading up to this week. It was coming up to the final dramatic clashes with Jerusalem's religious elite.

Before we get to the parable, let's take a bit more time looking at what had been happening in Jerusalem. The day before, Jesus had made his entrance into the holy city, celebrated by huge noisy crowds who tore branches off trees to make a carpet to welcome him. Not stopping, he'd marched right through the city to the temple. Arriving there with his crowd he drove away the market traders, tipped tables over, shouted accusations and – possibly even more annoyingly to the temple leaders – performed miraculous healings, *showing his power*, before ending his day at a lodge outside the city in Bethany.

All this meant, in the morning, when Jesus arrived at the temple to start teaching, it wasn't exactly surprising he was confronted by the chief priests and elders. To say they were feeling a little *prickly* would be an understatement. (I like to picture the mess from yesterday still being swept up in the background.)

These events frame the parable we're going to look at now. In it, there's a father (authority figure) and two sons. The father owns a vineyard and his sons are asked to do some work in it. Jesus' first hearers, both the temple leadership and the gathered crowd, will have known vineyard meant Israel, God's kingdom… therefore the father was a stand-in for God.

The plot twist is the seemingly obedient son who says the right things – "Yes, sir! Right away sir!" – but doesn't act on the promise he has made. He stays at home rather than going out in the heat to tend the vineyard.

The other son – the disobedient rude son, who tells his father "I will not!" – has a change of heart and gets on with the job. He bends to the authority of his father once he's had a chance to think.

There's a big difference between *people-pleasing* and *doing the right thing*. The son who said "yes" to his father's face didn't act on it when his father wasn't watching, so his response was superficial. The son who said "no" risked confrontation but afterwards he did the right thing and got on with what was asked.

Jesus had prepared the message of this parable when he miraculously killed that fig tree. It's no use having the appearance of a fig tree, being all fig wood and fig leaves, if you aren't producing figs. The *appearance* of obedience means nothing without the *fruit* of obedience. In the same way the temple and all the priests and elders and scribes had the *appearance* of obedience. But when the time came and Jesus was looking for "figs", they proved themselves pointless, and were therefore condemned. It had been no use sustaining the temple all these centuries, waiting for his arrival, if now that Jesus had arrived they ignored him because he was disruptive. In fact, it would have been better to have spent the years in disobedience – as a tax-collecting publican, or a sex-selling prostitute – and then see Jesus, and repent, than spending their time in the temple, promising everything, but be against him when he arrives.

So, instead of trying to calm things down a bit, Jesus used this missile of a parable to call judgement on the temple that morning.

Today the message is this. The father (God) calls all his sons. Many will respond, but some will be putting on a show; they will promise everything and end up delivering nothing. Others will be late converts. But, whatever else you've been doing up to now, it's better to be a late convert than to reject Jesus.

Questions for reflection:

Fig leaves are no good if the tree doesn't have figs. How might a Christian still miss the point, in the same way the Jewish temple leadership missed the point?

What might it look like to give a superficial "yes" but not follow through and "work in the vineyard"?

How is this parable encouraging to someone who has never yet had a relationship with the Lord?

One thing you can do

Since it's never too late to start obeying Jesus, next time you're talking to someone older than you, ask them about their relationship with God. How obedient they are being to their creator? Have they responded yet?

Part 3

The Shadow of the Cross

Jesus' Final Week

Jesus prepares his followers for the future.

"Not-a-Parable" of the Tyre Shop

A businessman bought a workshop on the edge of town, and he renovated it, painted the floors, and fitted it out with tyre changing equipment and car ramps. He purchased all the necessary tools, sparing no expense. He employed staff and put an experienced manager in charge of it all. Then he went away to live in the sun.

At the end of the first tax year, the businessman sent over a member of staff to check up on his tyre shop and collect a return on his investment. But at the tyre shop they were obstructive and wouldn't let him in. Another member of staff arrived to try again, but they blocked him; there was a stand-off. This time it turned nasty, and he ended up badly beaten. A third man was sent to try to reason with them, but this man never returned.

Finally, the businessman called his beloved son and said, "Please go to my tyre shop and collect a return on my investment." The man thought they would respect his son, but when the tyre shop saw him coming, they said to one another, "This is the heir, let's kill him and then everything will be ours."

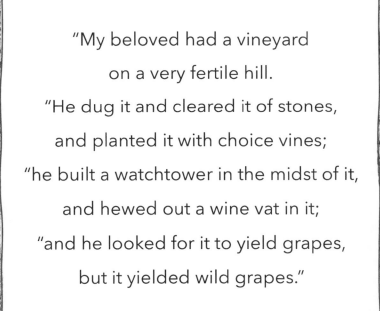

"My beloved had a vineyard
on a very fertile hill.
"He dug it and cleared it of stones,
and planted it with choice vines;
"he built a watchtower in the midst of it,
and hewed out a wine vat in it;
"and he looked for it to yield grapes,
but it yielded wild grapes."

Isaiah 5:1-2

22 Respect My Son

The Wicked Tenants

Matthew 21:33-46

Hear another parable. There was a master of a house who planted a vineyard and put a fence around it and dug a winepress in it and built a tower and leased it to tenants, and went into another country. When the season for fruit drew near, he sent his servants to the tenants to get his fruit. And the tenants took his servants and beat one, killed another, and stoned another. Again he sent other servants, more than the first. And they did the same to them. Finally he sent his son to them, saying, "They will respect my son." But when the tenants saw the son, they said to themselves, "This is the heir. Come, let us kill him and have his inheritance."

The basic principle of business investment is a simple one, and it remains simple no matter how complicated the actual business is. There are tenants or employees who get on with the work. While they earn a living, the owner or investor collects a share. If it all goes well it should be a win–win.

But to a business investor, what do you think makes a good tenant?

If I had invested in a vineyard – which, for the record, I've not – I'd like to see the vines well-tended and watered. That sounds like a good start. I'd like to see the weeds removed, the fences and tower maintained properly and the winepress kept tidy. I'd like to be confident all this would still be happening if I were away. Finally, when harvest time came I'd hope for my share of the profits, to repay all my time and expense. I'd be hoping for a return on my investment. That's how these things usually work. If all this was happening I'd probably say my tenants were good.

On the other hand, if when harvest time came I sent my servants and they were beaten and killed, I'd start to have serious misgivings about my tenants. And if I sent my beloved son to collect the harvest and he was ambushed and beaten to death? These murderers would face judgement for their treatment of my servants and son.

It sounds like an extreme story, but it wasn't simply fiction; it's a *God's eye view* of what happened. The religious authorities of the day were the bad tenants. Entrusted with the leadership of Israel,[51] they had kept the place looking nice and carefully looked after themselves. Unfortunately, because they were enjoying the boss's absence and wanted to stay in power, they were also silencing and abusing any prophets who spoke up against them. Profits came before prophets, you might say. Now Jesus, who was God's beloved son, was speaking against them – and it wouldn't be long before they'd kill him as well.

What will the owner of the vineyard do? He will destroy the tenants and give the vineyard to others (verse 8).

This story was aimed at the leadership of the day, and we could spend plenty of time thinking how shameful these first-century religious

---

[51] The meaning of the "vineyard".

leaders were. But probably it would be more useful for us to ask: what sort of vineyard tenants *are we*?

We'd like to answer the good sort. We'd be keeping the vines pruned and the winepress working. We'd be stewarding the owner's resources, sending him his share, and obedient to his staff. But, even if we start off with good intentions, we must careful we don't make the same mistakes.

Did you notice in the parable that at first the tenants were trying to avoid paying the owner his share, but by the time the son arrives they were plotting to get their hands on the whole vineyard? See how their rebellion grew? It grew in greed; from resisting a tithe to grasping the whole vineyard. It grew in rebellion: from a beating to murder and ultimately to the murder of the son.

Like the bad tenants, we might start off small, sending the first servant home empty-handed. But the rebellion grows. Although total rejection might seem a long way off, *compromise* is the road that leads there. One day we're cutting corners, skipping things we don't think really matter. Our discipleship becomes a bit less wholehearted; we miss prayer meetings, or skip a Sunday gathering. Good habits you once worked hard to keep become less regular, like Bible reading, mealtime grace, or prayer journalling, perhaps; you become disconnected. As good habits are broken you discover bad habits creeping in – forgotten sins reemerge, old patterns of thought come back. You start to break your relationship with the vineyard owner, and subtly claim the vineyard for yourself.

Thus, we arrive at a place where we say, "This is the heir. Come, let us kill him and the inheritance will be ours." God must be dead; kill Jesus too and we will have everything to ourselves.

Although the message of the parable was first for the temple leadership, we have the same question to face. Just like them, in *our* tenancy, only one thing will matter. We are judged as good or bad based on how we react to God's beloved son Jesus, when he arrives to collect the harvest. And the parable makes it clear that, if we're against God's son, we won't be staying in the vineyard.

Questions for reflection:

Killing God's son shows a complete rejection of God's plan for salvation; what attitude might be the equivalent of sending the first servant home empty-handed?

In this parable we learn that not all of God's "tenants" are good ones. What might it look like to be a bad tenant today?

What is the crucial difference between a good tenant and a bad one?

One thing you can do

Believers aren't simply hanging around waiting for Jesus to come some day in the future. There is plenty of work to do now. Check your habits today, so that you aren't losing track of the small things that lead to big problems.

23 No (Good) Excuses

The Great Supper

Luke 14:15-24

A man once gave a great banquet and invited many. And at the time for the banquet he sent his servant to say to those who had been invited, "Come, for everything is now ready." But they all alike began to make excuses. The first said to him, "I have bought a field, and I must go out and see it. Please have me excused." And another said, "I have bought five yoke of oxen, and I go to examine them. Please have me excused." And another said, "I have married a wife, and therefore I cannot come." So the servant came and reported these things to his master. Then the master of the house became angry and said to his servant, "Go out quickly to the streets and lanes of the city, and bring in the poor and crippled and blind and lame." And the servant said, "Sir, what you commanded has been done, and still there is room." And the master said to the servant, "Go out to the highways and hedges and compel people to come in, that my house may be filled. For I tell you, none of those men who were invited shall taste my banquet."

Luke 14:1–24 is one continuous narrative about a time when Jesus went to dine at the home of a leading Pharisee. From the details we have, it looks like Jesus spoiled the event for them, or at least, he wasn't exactly the dream guest. Remember we said that Jesus wasn't preoccupied with being nice? This dinner is a good example of that...

From the outset, according to Luke 14:1, Jesus was being *watched carefully*. Even so, he picked out a man with dropsy and asked the lawyers if it would be legal to heal him on the sabbath. Not getting an answer, Jesus healed the man anyway. Then Jesus watched everyone choosing the best places to sit,[52] and suggested it would be better to sit in the lowest places and wait till you're invited to move up the table. (i.e. be more humble). Finally Jesus told the host he probably should have fed the poor and crippled, instead of all his friends, relatives and rich neighbours, since it isn't real generosity if you'll just get an invite back another day.

So, overall, Jesus wasn't offering a lesson on winning friends.

One of the guests reclining at the table, who, given what's been going on so far, probably wanted to break the tension, announced, "Blessed is everyone who will eat bread in the Kingdom of God!" It sounds like the sort of thing nobody could argue with. But for Jesus it is an opportunity to teach a little about *who*, exactly, will be eating bread in the Kingdom of God. It was at *this* point that Jesus told this short story, the parable of the Great Supper.

The story begins with a man who has invited many people to a great banquet. By "many" and "great" we should imagine this is a big event, not a little tea party. He will have prepared for it, inviting his

---

[52] Seating yourselves according to social rank was the norm.

guests far in advance. Think of our modern "save the date" cards. This is a grand celebration coming up. He has invested in it.

When the big day comes he sends out his servant to bring everyone in, but the invited guests all make lame excuses. They put everyday concerns like property purchases, livestock inspections and hanging out with new wives above the massive celebratory feast that they have been invited to. It's like calling your mum on her eightieth birthday and saying you can't come to the party because you've booked a test drive in a mid-spec Toyota[53] hatchback. Here, common and everyday concerns have trumped a rare festivity.

The master, becoming angry, sends out his servant to find new guests, ones who will show a bit more interest. First they search the lanes and streets of the city. This is where you'd find the poor and destitute, disabled and diseased, people from the fringes of first-century Jewish society. Secondly they search the hedgerows and highways, the places outside the city of Jerusalem, where you find the true outsiders, the non-Jewish, the Samaritans and gentiles.

Having now filled his house with these new people, the master announces that "none of those men who were invited shall taste my banquet".

That's the story Jesus told around the table at this dinner party, in the fancy home of a leading Pharisee. Jesus' meaning would have been understood. The great banquet was a symbol for the Kingdom of God. The master of the house was therefore a stand-in for God. The servant perhaps a messenger? Or maybe even Jesus?

---

[53] I've got nothing against Toyota.

Jesus was teaching that even the people who had held "save the date" cards for generations, God's chosen people of Israel, can lose their place at the great banquet if they give lame excuses to the servant of God when the day comes. If they put the everyday *temporary* journey above the final *eternal* destination, they have got their priorities upside down and it will cost them. Whatever the excuses are, they are all lame compared to the eternal feast that has been prepared.

Back then, this message was directed at the Jewish temple leaders, who were around the table, along with their friends and colleagues. These leaders would have seen themselves as the invited guests of the parable, waiting for the banquet to begin.

Suppose Jesus turned up today and told this story at our party. Who might see themselves as the invited guests? Would it be us? Our pastors? Our bishops?

There is no room for complacency around the dinner table in God's kingdom. God has extended his invitation to all, sent out his messengers far and wide. Heaven will be filled with people who accept the invitation *and* turn up, ready to gratefully accept what's on offer. Lame excuses anger God. If we put something else above this, assuming we can turn up later, we will miss out on the greatest invitation ever sent.

Let's get personal. Do you have somewhere else you'd rather end up? What might be your excuse? A new car or house, an investment or holiday? It could be anything coming between you and *obeying God's word*. If it's becoming more important to you than your creator, then put it back in its proper place, or get rid of it completely. Your sport is causing you to miss church? Lame excuse; find a way to turn up and be a part of God's family, or it's likely you'll begin to drift. Your iPhone is distracting you from prayer or scripture? Lame excuse; throw it out the window if you need to. This invitation is too important to risk distraction. Put it like this: on judgement day you'll feel silly explaining to Jesus that you chose a smartphone over his eternity.

We are warned, having received our invitation, not to let *temporary* trivial distractions get in the way of us turning up when the day comes.

Questions for reflection:

If God told you the world was ending in fifteen mins and you could ask him to delay it a bit, would you?

Why? If you would – what would the reason be?

Is that more important than the wrapping up of all time and entry into the eternal Kingdom of God?

How can we live in the shadow of the greatest "save the date" card ever issued, ensuring we're ready to turn up when the day comes?

One thing you can do

Give up something that generally distracts you from time with your creator – something menial that intrudes into your devotional or prayer time, or cuts into your Bible reading. Perhaps social media, or smartphones with a news feed... Give it up for a week and see what the knock-on effect is. Hopefully this will convince you and lead to a long-term improvement in your relationship with God.

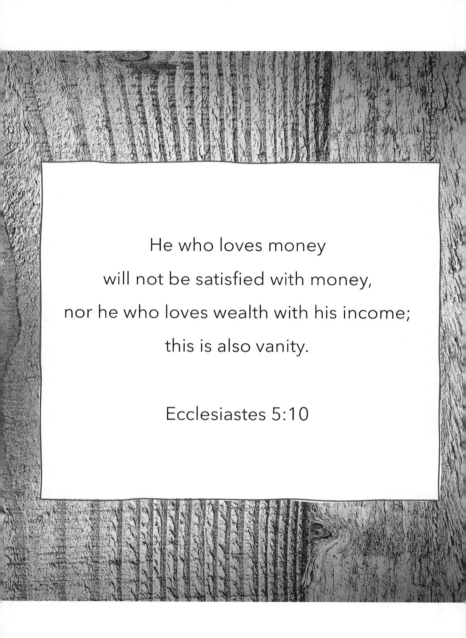

He who loves money
will not be satisfied with money,
nor he who loves wealth with his income;
this is also vanity.

Ecclesiastes 5:10

24 Learn from Jeff

The Dishonest Manager

Luke 16:1-9

He also said to the disciples, "There was a rich man who had a manager, and charges were brought to him that this man was wasting his possessions. And he called him and said to him, 'What is this that I hear about you? Turn in the account of your management, for you can no longer be manager.' And the manager said to himself, 'What shall I do, since my master is taking the management away from me? I am not strong enough to dig, and I am ashamed to beg. I have decided what to do, so that when I am removed from management, people may receive me into their houses.' So, summoning his master's debtors one by one, he said to the first, 'How much do you owe my master?' He said, 'A hundred measures of oil.' He said to him, 'Take your bill, and sit down quickly and write fifty.' Then he said to another, 'And how much do you owe?' He said, 'A hundred measures of wheat.' He said to him, 'Take your bill, and write eighty.' The master commended the dishonest manager for his shrewdness. For the sons of this world are more shrewd in dealing with their own generation than the sons of light. And I tell you, make friends for yourselves by means of unrighteous wealth, so that when it fails they may receive you into the eternal dwellings."

Jeff Bezos, one of the richest men of our generation, apparently only has one outfit in his wardrobe, to save his "decision energy" for business. Billionaire Elon Musk sleeps in his office, quite regularly, apparently. Whatever else you might say about them, both these people, and many others like them, are completely dedicated to the businesses they run.

The business world of Jesus' day is the backdrop to this parable, a world familiar to his first listeners, but for us it requires a bit of a history lesson. At this time there was a *huge* divide between the rich and the poor.[54] There was nobody much in between, not like we call the middle classes today. By a series of cunning legalistic workarounds, a small number of powerful people had grown rich and monopolised the promised land. When the Bible describes somebody as a "rich man", think of a super-wealthy elite landowner.

The *closest* thing to a middle class in that day would be servants on the upper rungs of the rich's payroll. The top servants. Among these were the agents, merchants and managers who were trusted to deal, and trade with, the affairs of the rich. These were educated people who could write, calculate and administrate. While they weren't rich like their employers, they still had a few more comforts than regular people.

---

[54] Despite God's rules given through Moses, that, if followed, would have prevented such inequalities.

The characters we meet in the parable are the corrupt sons of this world. The manager is dishonest, and we can see that by his behaviour. The merchants are no better; they go along with the scheme because it benefits them. Even the rich man, when he finds out, doesn't exactly condemn any of it. It's all part of a crooked game. Nobody is keeping God's law. Welcome to the dishonest arena of worldly trade; and funnily enough, it hasn't changed much in the last 2000 years.

As the story plays out, the manager discovers he is about to be fired for wasting his boss' money and is given a deadline to wrap up his accounts. Realising his comfortable life is hanging by a thread, and fearing hard labour or begging on the street, he thinks of a way to buy himself a future. Since he's still in charge of the accounts for now, he starts doing a few favours... He's cheating his boss, but he's already getting fired, right?

So he calls the merchants in and gets them to rewrite their accounts to lower debts, which they do gladly. When his boss finds out, he seems to shrug it off. He wouldn't be pleased to have been cheated but he still commends the manager for his shrewd behaviour. Perhaps he realised it was a mistake to leave the man in control knowing he was leaving. Perhaps he hadn't thought of it himself, so he was impressed by the cleverness. Either way, in this crooked game the dishonest manager just scored a point.

Jesus explains the meaning of the parable like this: "For the sons of this world are more shrewd in dealing with their own generation than the *sons of light*." We could say: look at how these worldly people deal with each other, and learn from how eagerly they pursue what they desire. The *sons of light*, likewise, should be single-minded in putting their resources to good use. Jesus clarifies his meaning by adding, "Make friends for yourself by means of unrighteous wealth, so that when it fails, they may receive you into the eternal dwellings." Wealth, which is unrighteous, is a temporary state, will pass away and "fail". Nevertheless, what we do now in this temporary world can be used to secure an eternal future.

Therefore, in this jarring and explosive parable, Jesus teaches that we are to be like the dishonest manager in the way he single-mindedly used whatever resources he had – in this case wealth – to secure his future. We are not supposed to copy the dishonest manager in other ways. (Not, for instance, his dishonesty.)

He tells us that the single-mindedness, often found among businessmen who love money, should be copied by Christians in their pursuit of the Kingdom of Heaven.

This is how Jesus is using people like our Jeff and Elon to set an example to us. I find this quite challenging. How about you? Are you as dedicated to following Jesus as these people are to chasing money?

Questions for reflection:

Worldly people can still make good examples, even if they would be terrible heroes… How can we learn from worldly people without worshipping them?

Think about the things you naturally go "all in" for. What are they?

How would it change your relationship with Jesus if you could chase after the Kingdom of Heaven with the same vigour?

One thing you can do

Learn about some successful business owners – perhaps think of a business you admire (or love to hate) and research the people behind it – They're not necessarily people you want to copy. Weigh up what you find out – Jesus says their business shrewdness or dedication to money is something we can learn from and apply to our discipleship.

25 The Great Divorce

The Rich Man and Lazarus

Luke 16:19-31

There was a rich man who was clothed in purple and fine linen and who feasted sumptuously every day. And at his gate was laid a poor man named Lazarus, covered with sores, who desired to be fed with what fell from the rich man's table. Moreover, even the dogs came and licked his sores. The poor man died and was carried by the angels to Abraham's side. The rich man also died and was buried, and in Hades, being in torment, he lifted up his eyes and saw Abraham far off and Lazarus at his side. And he called out, "Father Abraham, have mercy on me, and send Lazarus to dip the end of his finger in water and cool my tongue, for I am in anguish in this flame." But Abraham said, "Child, remember that you in your lifetime received your good things, and Lazarus in like manner bad things; but now he is comforted here, and you are in anguish. And besides all this, between us and you a great chasm has been fixed, in order that those who would pass from here to you may not be able, and none may cross from there to us." And he said, "Then I beg you, father, to send him to my father's house—for I have five brothers—so that he may warn them, lest they also come into this place of torment." But

Abraham said, "They have Moses and the Prophets; let them hear them." And he said, "No, father Abraham, but if someone goes to them from the dead, they will repent." He said to him, "If they do not hear Moses and the Prophets, neither will they be convinced if someone should rise from the dead."

For years my morning walk took me under the same tree. A big, beautiful tree that hung dramatically over the footpath. One day I reached this tree and a huge bough, nearly a metre[55] thick, had broken off and landed where I usually walk, crushing a fence flat and completely blocking the path. It turned out all along the tree had been completely rotten, and every morning I could have been squashed as flat as the fence now was... Sometimes we are offered these reminders[56] that life is finite – it can end at any point. This is what happens in the parable of the rich man and Lazarus; they both die. Jesus has a lesson to teach us about their fortunes afterwards.

If you thought Jesus was a soft touch, getting to know this parable should help change that. Because, while a parable like the Lost Sheep might fill us with comforting picture-book visions of a softly spoken, fluffy-bearded shepherd from Oxfordshire lovingly carrying his lamb home,[57] you can't deny this parable he told is unsettling and full of chilly warning. After teaching about seeking the lost, mission, and

---

[55] Apologies if you don't like metric – that's about two long cubits.

[56] Most people I know can think *of* one. But I'm not certain we like to think *about* them.

[57] The sort of picture you find on an Oxfordshire stained-glass church window.

redemption – with the parables of the Lost Sheep, the Lost Coins and the Prodigal Son – Jesus changes his tone completely and reminds us that *the law is the law*, and judgement is real: "it is easier for heaven and earth to pass away than for one dot of the law to become void" (verse 17).

Here Jesus presents two contrasting men, on one hand an unnamed rich man, dressed in purple – the expensive colour of royalty – living in a fine home full of the best things he can buy, feasting every day; on the other hand there's the poor man he's ignoring, called Lazarus, covered in pustulating sores, licked by filthy dogs, laid starving to death at the rich man's gate. He's in a condition so revolting even reading this description makes me feel like I need a wash.

When they both die, the rich man is laid to rest, buried carefully. The poor man has his feeble body thrown outside of the city to rot away.

Yet from now on their fortunes are reversed. Lazarus – whose name means *who God helps* – is carried to heaven to sit with Abraham. The rich man, who poignantly remains unnamed, sinks to Hell and torment. And, despite his pleading, he remains there. Accustomed to being important in the world, he tries to persuade Abraham to send Lazarus to comfort him with water. He's still behaving like he holds influence… but that world is gone!

Abraham explains it's not possible. And what's more, he won't send Lazarus to warn the rich man's brothers either. If they don't repent, they'll be joining the rich man in torment. Why? Because if they won't listen to Moses (the law) and they won't listen to the prophets either (God's messengers) then they aren't going to repent when old dog-licked Lazarus turns up from the dead to suggest they change their ways.

By disobeying God's[58] commands the rich man has brought a permanent judgement on himself and is excluded from the Kingdom of Heaven. For Jesus' original listeners this might have been shocking. The rich were surely *blessed* by God, so how could they end up in eternal torment while the poor are exalted into the company of Abraham and the Angels? Surely this isn't the way of God's kingdom.

What does this story mean for us today?

The lesson is unchanged from then to now. Like Lazarus, those *who God helps* are destined for heaven and entrance into God's eternal presence. Like the rich man, eventually those who don't repent will run out of time, there will be no more chances.

But the story finishes like this: because of God's multiple revelations to us we can't plead ignorance. Because of the evidence in creation, we have no excuse. Because of the law laid out in the books of Moses (the first five books of the Bible), we have no excuse. Because of the warnings of the many prophets, who have spoken his word to us all, throughout history, we have no excuse. And crucially, because of the final revelation through the coming of Jesus Christ, his teaching, and ultimately his resurrection from the dead confirming his authority, we are completely and utterly without excuse.

---

[58] Revealed by his selfishness – as he allowed Lazarus to starve to death at his gates, while he enjoyed his excesses in luxurious surroundings.

Death will come to us; whether slowly and predictably after a long life, or suddenly and unexpectedly. By that point, if we haven't repented it will be too late. There will be a separation, with an uncrossable barrier, and if we haven't listened to the warnings by then there will be no use pleading.

Questions for reflection:

Are we taking the law seriously and heading the warning for ourselves?

What will bring us shame when we look back from Heaven or Hell? i.e. is there a "beggar on our doorstep" who needs our help?

When the rich man found himself in torment, realising there was nothing more he could do to save himself, his thoughts turned to his family still on earth. Unlike him, if you're reading this now it isn't too late to warn our family and friends and neighbours. Are we taking seriously our mission to warn "our brothers"?

One thing you can do

Warn someone about the future. Ask if they have considered that they won't live on earth forever, and tell them what Jesus said: the decisions they make in life will have everlasting consequences.

"Not-a-Parable" of the Gardener

If you employ a man to look after your garden, you don't do it for him. Would you get the mower our and drive it for him while he sits down and rests? Would you empty the grass box into the compost and sweep up? If he's weeding the flowerbeds, do you follow him around picking them up and taking them away?

Will you thank him graciously for every little thing he picks up and moves, every part of the job he does that you have paid him to do?

And after the work is done and the garden is looking smart, do you lay a table on the patio and light the BBQ? And will you sit him down with a plate of food before your family and give him a cold beer to drink?

No... he turns up, whether you are at home or not, and he does his work as planned. Then once it's finished you might politely thank him, and he'll say, "No worries," and you'll send him away with the money you agreed on.

26 Do Your Duty

The Unworthy Servant

Luke 17:7–10

Will any one of you who has a servant ploughing or keeping sheep say to him when he has come in from the field, "Come at once and recline at table"? Will he not rather say to him, "Prepare supper for me, and dress properly, and serve me while I eat and drink, and afterwards you will eat and drink"? Does he thank the servant because he did what was commanded? So you also, when you have done all that you were commanded, say, "We are unworthy servants; we have only done what was our duty."

My wife and I hired a cleaner once, which was really helpful for a while. She kept the house beautifully clean for us, during a time of our lives when we were both busy working and parenting our three young children. But, because I wasn't used to having anyone working for us in the house, I found it difficult to be home when she was working. It was nothing to do with our cleaner, who was lovely; it was because I found it hard to rest, or get on with what I was supposed to be doing while she was cleaning. I wanted to jump up and help, or thank her for every small part of her job. "The bin… thank you, that's so kind… the window… thank you…" I suspect she found it off-putting. In fact it's more than a suspicion; she'd often remind me we were paying her to do those things and I should stop getting in the way.

Jesus told this parable to a private audience of his disciples. His disciples were his students, he was the teacher, and part of that custom also meant being a servant to his needs. They would meet commands like, "collect that donkey", "prepare me a boat", "distribute this bread". Being a servant was part of the learning. So when Jesus started talking about servants in this story, the gathered disciples will have known Jesus had his eyes on them.

The story is simple enough. Jesus asked who, with a servant, would expect to wait on them? Would they expect to call the servant in and prepare a meal for them? It certainly wasn't the custom. When the field work was done, the servant came in, got changed, and fixed a meal for the boss before settling down later with food and drink for himself.

It is the natural order of things. A servant does not expect to be waited on by his master, nor does the master expect to spend his day catering for his servants.

The same applies, Jesus teaches, when God is your boss. We need to have in our hearts "We are unworthy servants; we only have done what is our duty." That's not to be grovelling (to our informal ears the language can sound phoney today) but because it's a straightforward *statement of a fact*.

To talk about "unworthiness" is not false humility; it's genuine knowing-your-place-ness. Literally meaning *not worthy of*, in the sense of "I am not deserving of special thanks because I am meant to serve, and I have no other purpose in being here today." It's meant in the same sense my cleaner would correct me.

None of this is to suggest that any of us should be ungrateful, or thankless when we speak, whether that's up or down the chain of command. Gracious interactions with staff, waiters, shop assistants, managers and bosses are good practice! No, what it means is, learning from the everyday example Jesus gives us, we should correctly understand our places. Our attitude towards our Lord and master should match the example of the servant. Part of what we do, is serve.

So we mustn't approach kingdom work as though we are offering to do God a favour. It's easy to get confused here; perhaps it's because so many of us volunteer for our churches, and that means we can see kingdom work as doing our church family a favour, as though it's not our "real" work, and treat it very differently to the work we get paid for with money. But should you serve God with the kind of attitude you'd normally have if you're helping a friend move house: *as a favour*, something on the side...? If you do, you probably won't be able to keep it up. There's only a certain number of times you feel happy to do that... especially if they forget to thank you or fail to offer you tea or cake during the process. If you take this attitude you will reach your limit at some point, whatever your temperament. But remember this is kingdom work and I think you'll have a better chance.

To be a good and faithful servant, like a good employee, you need to have your heart in the right place. When it comes to serving God, our attitude needs to match the reality; Jesus is your master, your "boss", not just a friend you volunteer to help with something.

Jesus, of course, *did* describe himself in other ways too. For instance, he came to serve and give his life as a ransom, and was friend to his disciples, as well as a master. So Jesus is at the same time the king and master we serve, our friend, our saviour, and our example to follow while we serve… These are strands we need to twist together when we read this parable. If you've ever had the privilege of working happily together with friends, or under a hardworking leader who is also a friend, or family, then perhaps you have a taste of the picture of serving that Jesus is painting. I have – in business, my wife, Francine, and I worked together for many years, and on top of that, many of our employees became friends too, and these were some of the happiest workdays of our lives.

"But what about my employer, the person who gives me money in exchange for my labour?" I hear you ask. Or people like the prime minister? How do they fit into the picture? These are temporary powers in this world. We aren't supposed to go around making trouble for them, but we need to remember they aren't truly in charge; Jesus is. And all Jesus' commands are commands from your heavenly "boss".

The message is: we are supposed to work for him and serve his kingdom. Taking this seriously should be our expectation and our attitude. Knowing he is also our friend, our saviour and perfect example should make this a great pleasure as well, but we are only doing our duty.

Questions for reflection:

As an employee (a servant in the world), do you obey the rules and regulations set out by your boss? Even if you aren't convinced how useful they are?

Are their consequences if you fail to?

Do you have a similar attitude to God's laws?

How does this story help us to put Jesus first at all times?

One thing you can do

Make yourself a little sign that says "Jesus is my master" and keep it somewhere handy - like your desk, or in your bag – so you'll be reminded when you have to make decisions.

27 Keep Praying

The Persistent Widow

Luke 18:1-8

And he told them a parable to the effect that they ought always to pray and not lose heart. He said, "In a certain city there was a judge who neither feared God nor respected man. And there was a widow in that city who kept coming to him and saying, 'Give me justice against my adversary.' For a while he refused, but afterwards he said to himself, 'Though I neither fear God nor respect man, yet because this widow keeps bothering me, I will give her justice, so that she will not beat me down by her continual coming.' And the Lord said, 'Hear what the unrighteous judge says. And will not God give justice to his elect, who cry to him day and night? Will he delay long over them? I tell you, he will give justice to them speedily. Nevertheless, when the Son of Man comes, will he find faith on earth?'"

Luke did something a little unusual in the way he framed this little parable, because he gave the whole point of the parable away at the beginning. The punchline is right at the start; if this were a joke it would be ruined... but it isn't a joke, and helpfully it means we can be really clear about the reason Jesus told this story, which was "to the effect that they ought to pray, and not lose heart." To fight the temptation to lose our confidence in prayer. To encourage us to pray to God in full assurance that he hears us and will act on our prayers.

In this explosive parable which overturns the expectations of the day, we meet a judge, who doesn't care about God at all, nor, by extension, God's laws. The rules of his creator do not bother him, not even in the slightest. He doesn't respect man either, which flows from his attitude to God. After all, if we don't respect God, why respect people who he made in his own image? So, he doesn't care about God, God's law, or God's image. What we have in this judge is an entirely selfish individual. If it doesn't affect him, his comfort or wellbeing, he isn't bothered.

We also meet a widow. We don't know much about her but a widow was on a pretty low rung in society back then. She was at the mercy of everyone else. Widows were vulnerable, since it was hard to survive without the care of a husband. But for the time being let's assume she's doing ok, apart from a legal dispute of some kind.[59]

Her trouble is that the judge won't pass a judgement for her. Perhaps it's just more convenient for him to side with her opponent, probably a man with greater standing in the community. Perhaps her opponent is a friend of the judge, but, even if not, it's likely to be someone who matters more to the judge than she does. Or perhaps, because it doesn't benefit him, the judge just can't be bothered to deal with the case of the vulnerable widow. She simply doesn't matter enough.

---

[59] Which may or may not be related to the loss of her husband and his estate.

Despite the knockbacks, our widow is persistent in making a nuisance of herself, and eventually it pays off. He is worn down by it, and fears she will *beat him down* by turning up in his law court every day. So, therefore, he gives her the justice she desires, if only so she'll leave him alone.

So what does this mean? Firstly, something it doesn't mean – it doesn't mean God is a reluctant judge, who doesn't care about people. God doesn't answer prayers thinking, "Now perhaps she'll leave me alone!"

What Jesus is telling us is that, if *even* a selfish, godless judge will grant a request to a lowly widow, for persistent asking, *how much more* will God grant the prayers of his elect? If even this rotten man will do it, *how much more* can you trust God to? So don't lose heart. God will grant these things and when he does it will happen speedily, suddenly. A time will come when you can look back and say – really knowing it – all my prayers have been truly heard and answered; none were ever ignored or forgotten.

The testy question Jesus ends on is this: when the Son of Man comes, will he find faith on earth? Will we have lost hope in God by the time the Son of Man returns? Or, like the widow, will we be praying persistently without losing heart?

Questions for reflection:

We have impatient hearts, and the fact Jesus taught this parable tells us it's nothing new: God is familiar with our impatient hearts. Are you prone to giving up on your prayers?

What can make you lose heart, or what fills you with hope and encouragement in your prayer life?

How does this parable encourage you?

One thing you can do

Put this parable into action. What is your most frequent prayer? Commit to it and make it a habit to pray regularly for this one thing.

"Not-a-Parable" of the Pastor's Prayer

A pastor approached the lectern, lifted his arms in prayer, and began, with his microphone on, "My Dear Lord, as I look around this church, I see these other men and women who pretend to love you. I see self-righteous rich men who drive fancy German cars. I see covetous women coming through your doors still logged onto Instagram. I see cheaters, liars, deceivers. For example, David, on the back row, is a complete hypocrite since he took that busy new job in IT and dropped off the hospitality team.

"Half the people in this room don't even tithe properly. Unlike them, I am careful to give 10 per cent of my wages — before taxes and expenses. And I give more on top of that. I get up an hour before any of them to pray. And I attend the evening service *as well as* the morning service every week. You are lucky to have me, Lord, and I thank you, earnestly, that I am not like anyone else here. Amen."

Meanwhile David, on the back row, sat quietly praying in his heart for forgiveness.

28 God, Have Mercy On Me!

The Pharisee and the Tax Collector

Luke 18:9–14

He also told this parable to some who trusted in themselves that they were righteous, and treated others with contempt: "Two men went up into the temple to pray, one a Pharisee and the other a tax collector. The Pharisee, standing by himself, prayed thus: "God, I thank you that I am not like other men, extortioners, unjust, adulterers, or even like this tax collector. I fast twice a week; I give tithes of all that I get." But the tax collector, standing far off, would not even lift up his eyes to heaven, but beat his breast, saying, "God, be merciful to me, a sinner!" I tell you, this man went down to his house justified, rather than the other. For everyone who exalts himself will be humbled, but the one who humbles himself will be exalted."

I used to be *so* proud, but thankfully I'm *much better* than that now… This is a joke I'm quite proud of. (Although nobody seems to get it…)

The human heart is very broken. Even if we know God's law and make an effort to follow it, we notice our improvement, and start feeding a sin more dangerous than what we had before. This sin is pride, and self-righteousness is what it creates. Our deceptive hearts whisper to us, "I see you doing good. You are *like God now*." It's easy to slip up like this. Perhaps we are never more than one *compliment* away from becoming a monster, if we fail to guard our hearts.

This is the condition of the people who Jesus spoke this parable to. We don't know their names, or their occupations, or whether they were gathered together on one occasion, or if this was a parable Jesus taught regularly to anyone who needed to hear. But we know they trusted in *their own righteousness*. By trusting in themselves for something only God can offer, they had put themselves on the same level as God. This is what we see in their attitude at prayer.

In the parable we meet two men praying who were in very different social positions. One was a Pharisee, exalted as a spiritual leader, in a position of respect and admiration. The other was a tax collector – a member of a hated profession – who extorted money from his fellow Jews to feed the vast machinery of the Roman occupiers. One exalted by his people; one hated.

The Pharisee, trusting that he was a good guy with his own righteousness, prays accordingly. He stands at the front, listing his achievements, and thanks God that he is unlike the others. Not only has he kept God's laws but also he has made hundreds more and kept them too. Not only has he fasted once a year (as required) but he has taken it upon himself to fast twice a week. Noticing what an awesome man he is, he thanks God. He's not asking for forgiveness because he doesn't think it's needed. His prayer is more like a performance for onlookers to marvel at than a heartfelt approach to God.

The tax collector, hated by his fellows as much as by himself, can't even find the confidence to approach the altar. Instead, he stands far off, perhaps as close as he dares to get. He can't look God in the face, so he keeps his eyes low. Rather than raise his hands to Heaven, he uses them to beat his aching heart in despair. Hopelessly he assesses his own predicament. He feels all the pain of a man condemned by God. "Be merciful to me, a sinner."

The bang in this parable is that the person who leaves justified is this sinful tax collector, because he pleas for the mercy he requires.

It's been said that trying to attain the holiness of God is like a man trying to reach for the sun. Failing, he climbs a stepladder and tries again. Perhaps he's four feet higher now, but he's no closer in any meaningful way. Likewise, the Pharisee, for all his fasting and tithing, has taken some action, yet he's only a man on a step reaching for the sun. But... worse, he's no longer humble, because he believes he has achieved something spectacular, and has raised himself over the others. From his stepladder he compares himself favourably to other people and looks down on them. Trusting in your own righteousness is like a broken pencil: pointless. And, painfully missing the point, the Pharisee no longer asks for the mercy he very much needs. And as a result he leaves the temple, no better off.

The one who exalts himself will be humbled. The one who humbles himself will be exalted.

Notice the Pharisee doesn't compare himself to the goodness of God, which would have humbled him? Instead he looks down on the tax collector in judgement. What a mistake...

It's good to be honest about ourselves, and our condition. Self-awareness is a good thing. Many Christian churches have a tradition of confession as part of every weekly service. I wonder if you've ever considered why. It's helpful if regularly, taking your lead from the tax collector, we confess our sins and reflect on them, asking for forgiveness, during prayer. The more often you do it, the more you'll recall your terrible thoughts, words and deeds. Don't excuse yourself, because that isn't helpful, but take a moment to consider them.

Sometimes a home group[60] within your church is a good place to confess sins and temptations. Building up a network of people who will hold you accountable is really valuable. You might consider a mentor, someone you can confide in and share what sins you're battling.

Build a habit of asking God for forgiveness. It's not required that you beat your chest, but if it helps you there's also no reason not to. Afterwards, look to Heaven. Take comfort that with repentance you can be forgiven, and you can leave justified, wearing not your own but Jesus' righteousness. That's a righteousness you can trust in.

---

[60] Or small group, connect group, life group, whatever you call them.

Questions for reflection:

Why is it tempting to be proud of our efforts to become righteous?

Why is this so dangerous?

Who can we trust in to forgive us, and leave us justified and fit for Heaven?

One thing you can do

Be alert to times you compare yourself to other people. Try and kick the habit.

Instead of comparing yourself to other broken people, compare yourself to God's perfection. Confess the ways you have missed the mark, asking for the forgiveness you need.

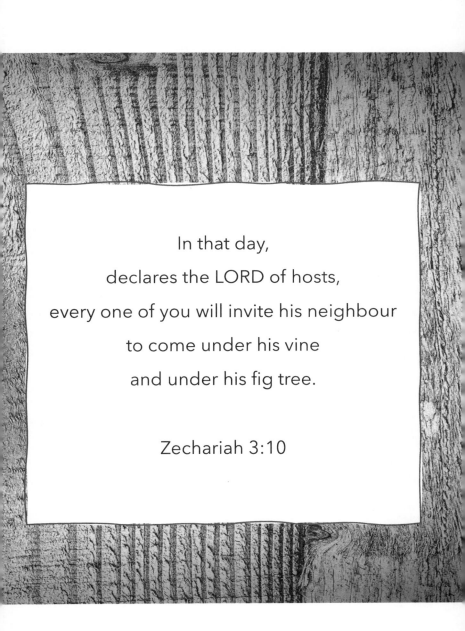

In that day,

declares the LORD of hosts,

every one of you will invite his neighbour

to come under his vine

and under his fig tree.

Zechariah 3:10

29 Heaven and Earth Will Pass Away

The Lesson of the Fig Tree

Mark 13:28-31

From the fig tree learn its lesson: as soon as its branch becomes tender and puts out its leaves, you know that summer is near. So also, when you see these things taking place, you know that he is near, at the very gates. Truly, I say to you, this generation will not pass away until all these things take place. Heaven and earth will pass away, but my words will not pass away.

I like figs. I like figs so much that a few years ago I planted a fig tree in the garden. I was looking forward to watching it grow and develop, and put out leaves and fruit. The first spring I watched carefully for the signs of new growth and tender branches. I was excited, but as soon as they did a rabbit[61] ate all the tender branches off. The plant died along with my dream of homegrown figs.

I suppose this rabbit had been watching for the same signs I had. My (negative) experience as a fig tree grower taught me to be more

---

[61] Or another hungry creature. I blamed the rabbit.

watchful. We need to watch out, even more attentively than rabbits watch for food.

This parable is part of a block of teaching Jesus gave his disciples shortly before his final arrest. In Matthew's Gospel there are many parables from this time, and we will consider more of these over the next few chapters. They have the same basic theme: the future. Jesus needed to prepare his disciples for what was coming. He warns them that worrying things will be going on around them, and he teaches them about what they mean, and how they should behave when it's happening. These lessons have remained relevant for each generation of Christians since Jesus, and they will still be relevant for every generation until Jesus returns in glory.

Let's turn to it then; Jesus draws our attention to the fig tree. The fig tree is different to most other trees[62] in Palestine because it drops its leaves in the winter. This makes it easy to spot the new buds starting to reappear when the warmer weather approaches.

Perhaps I'm overly poetic, but I find it fascinating that something as small as the little buds and branches, the tiny green flecks of leaf that appear in springtime, can be used to predict the appearance of something so big, and all encompassing, as the summer. Every year at springtime the landscape completely changes over just a few days when the hedges and grass put out their first shoots. Suddenly there's a transformation from muddy brown fields with bare trees and hedges, to the bright green of new growth. When it happens the weather is usually still fairly cold, damp and miserable. Yet... everything feels a bit different, because now we can see the first signs

---

[62] Trees such as the olive and carob hold onto their leaves.

of spring. The colours are different and bright. Summer, though it's still a long way off, is inevitably coming, its progress is unstoppable, and the early signs are all around us.

But not all signs mean *summer* is coming. Jesus warns his disciples to be on the lookout for different signs. Signs that mean "he is near, at the very gates". The signs Jesus talks about are found in verses 5–23. Look them up. They make concerning reading: false teachers, wars, rumours of wars, nation against nation, kingdom against kingdom, earthquakes and famines, persecution, brothers against brothers, fathers against their own children…

Some have tried to use this passage to predict when the end of the world will come, and they start counting earthquakes and keeping news articles. That's not going to be useful, given that these things have been going on ever since, and – this is the part the predictors skip over – even Jesus says he doesn't know when the end will come, only the Father knows that. So unless you have particular insight *that Jesus didn't*[63] – forget it. This parable isn't a roadmap to apocalypse. It's not about timing.[64]

Instead we should see these signs as evidence Heaven and earth won't last forever. Birthing pains, as Paul called them. So when we notice these signs we can be reminded of Jesus' words; "Heaven and earth will pass away." The skies, the stars, the earth we walk on, and the home you live in will all come to an end. That much has been

---

[63] You don't.

[64] Actually you can't do that with fig trees either – you can't measure the green shoots and forecast the day to get your paddling pool out.

made clear, "but my words will not pass away." It's as inevitable as summer arriving, at some point after the fig tree puts leaves out.

The lesson of Jesus' fig tree, then, is a bit like the lesson I learned from *my* fig tree. We must be aware, watchful, alert, prepared. But more importantly we keep our eyes on the *eternal* prize, knowing that Heaven and earth will pass away but Jesus' words will not pass away. We must cling to Jesus' eternal words, not our temporary home on earth.

If we take on board warnings like this we won't be caught unprepared. These signs can be used like the first appearance of spring: reminders that the world is temporary, and Jesus is coming. "He is near, at the very gates."

Questions for reflection:

To some people it might sound like a pretty bleak assessment of the future… but how can it encourage us that "Heaven and earth will pass away"?

How is it helpful to read the signs as Jesus suggests?

*Why might it **not** be helpful to try to predict the end of the world?*

One thing you can do

Watch the news thinking about what Jesus has said in this parable – but instead of trying to anticipate the end times, think about the fact that in this *temporary world* Jesus' words are an eternal feature; they "will not pass away".

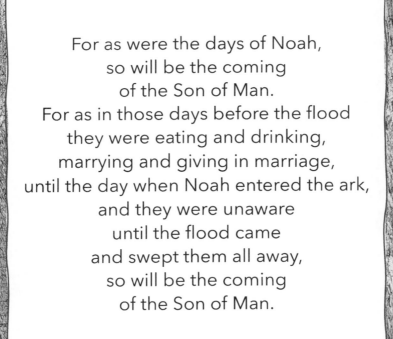

For as were the days of Noah,
so will be the coming
of the Son of Man.
For as in those days before the flood
they were eating and drinking,
marrying and giving in marriage,
until the day when Noah entered the ark,
and they were unaware
until the flood came
and swept them all away,
so will be the coming
of the Son of Man.

Matthew 24:37–39

30 Live in Expectation

The Householder and the Thief

Matthew 24:42-44

Therefore, stay awake, for you do not know on what day your Lord is coming. But know this, that if the master of the house had known in what part of the night the thief was coming, he would have stayed awake and would not have let his house be broken into. Therefore you also must be ready, for the Son of Man is coming at an hour you do not expect.

Some years ago it became popular among English thieves to crawl underneath vans and cut off the exhaust systems. They harvested them to sell the valuable parts for scrap. For the owner of the van the result was distressing – the vehicle couldn't be used and the cost to repair it was usually huge. To make matters worse, it was happening so often there was a shortage of replacement parts to fix them. I know about all this because at the time I was managing a fleet of vans. It was deeply frustrating. Especially since this was happening on our own property. Why couldn't we stop them? I genuinely considered how many nights I'd need to sleep outside before I caught someone in the act.

In Matthew 24–25 and Luke 12–13 we find Jesus teaching about the future. Jesus was approaching the cross, so his teaching had a new focus; equipping the disciples to "hang in there" once he left them.

Jesus gave fair warning to anyone who would listen, and practical advice for living between now and the end. He talked about the things that are coming, the final wrapping up of history.

Both Matthew and Luke record this short story about a homeowner who wouldn't have allowed his home to be burgled if he'd known when it was going to happen. He'd have stayed awake.

Pay attention to the word *therefore*. Jesus began by referring us back to what he was just speaking about. (Ask: what's the *therefore* there for…) He was speaking about warnings for the future, then he gave the Lesson of the Fig Tree, teaching us to be alert and watchful. Then his reminder of the days of Noah, who was saved by boarding the ark while everyone else was living normally.

Therefore, he said, given all these warnings I've just taught you about, stay awake, because *you don't know* when it's going to happen. The parable is about staying *spiritually* awake,[65] meaning readiness.

It goes without saying that a property owner who knows when the burglar is arriving will be ready to meet him and defend his property. Me too; although in the end I'd decided not to spend months living in a car park, if I had known which night the exhaust thief was arriving I'd have been there to stop him. Perhaps I'd meet him there with the police, or with a camera and something to defend myself with… I'm not exactly sure but I'd have been prepared.

---

[65] Not sleeplessness. For confirmation also read the Ten Virgins, which Matthew includes straight afterwards.

Jesus tells us that although these things *are* going to happen, we won't be told *when*.

We don't need to worry about why we aren't told when – but those who heed the warning will use the information we *are* given to be *prepared* for the future.

"*Therefore*, you must also be ready."

We need to be practical about preparing for what *has* been revealed to us. The householder couldn't expect to stay awake every night in case of burglars. It wouldn't work. Nor could I live on my driveway for the rest of my life.[66]

But it's perfectly normal to take measures to prepare for what's coming. For example, we lock our doors at night because we believe that the threat of burglary is genuine. If a storm is on the way we close our windows, tie things down, and put garden things away. When we *believe* that a threat is genuine, we do practical things is preparation.

Likewise if we *believe* what Jesus teaches us, we will take action to be prepared. We will make ourselves familiar with scripture, so we can take note of the warnings, and be prayerfully asking the Holy Spirit for understanding. We will seek to bear fruit like the fig tree – growing in our love of Jesus. We will be spiritually growing all the time, becoming more loving to strangers, more outspoken about our faith, more patient with our families, more generous with our finances and more sacrificial with our giving.

---

[66] Even if I did, my house would probably be burgled instead.

None of our Christian living can really be wholehearted if, as the foundation, you don't really believe one day Jesus will come back. And the day that happens we have been warned not to be caught unprepared, *spiritually asleep*.

That's what faith is, *believing* the warnings you were given, trusting the things you can't yet see, and then living like you are *awake* to them.

Questions for reflection:

Consider what Jesus said about Noah's generation in Matthew 24:38–39. What was the error of the generation?

What does it look like to fall asleep spiritually?

What would the consequences of this be?

One thing you can do

Build a massive ark like Noah did.

Actually, no, but do meditate on the effort Noah went to when God instructed him, and how his neighbours must have felt watching that thing go up.

How can you be prepared for the warnings Jesus has given us about the future?

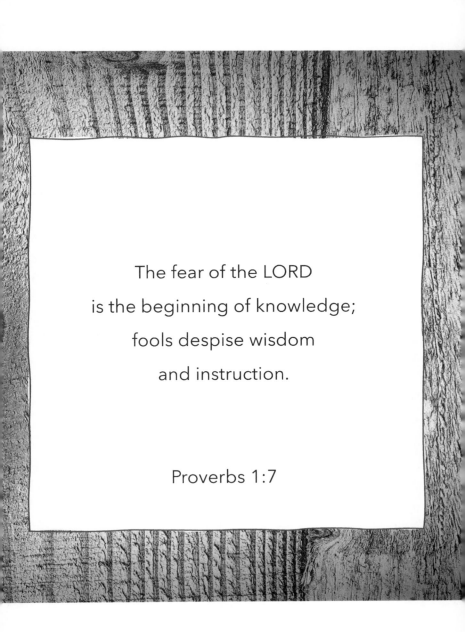

The fear of the LORD

is the beginning of knowledge;

fools despise wisdom

and instruction.

Proverbs 1:7

31 He Will Return

The Faithful and Unfaithful Servants

Matthew 24:45-51

Who then is the faithful and wise servant, whom his master has set over his household, to give them their food at the proper time? Blessed is that servant whom his master will find so doing when he comes. Truly, I say to you, he will set him over all his possessions. But if that wicked servant says to himself, "My master is delayed", and begins to beat his fellow servants and eats and drinks with drunkards, the master of that servant will come on a day when he does not expect him and at an hour he does not know and will cut him in pieces and put him with the hypocrites. In that place there will be weeping and gnashing of teeth.

I was once told about an experiment in a canteen, where an honesty box was set up on the counter, with a notice asking for donations. A week later the same box was still there but this time a *pair of eyes* was drawn over the notice, subtly reminding everyone they might be watched. The second week they collected twice the amount of money...

While you think you are being watched, doing the right thing is mostly about staying out of trouble. But your heart attitude is revealed by what you do when you think nobody is looking...

CS Lewis' book *The Screwtape Letters* has one demon writing to another, "Our cause is never more in danger than when a human, no longer desiring, but still intending to do our Enemy's will [God's will], looks around upon a universe from which every trace of Him [God] seems to have vanished, and asks why he has been forsaken, and still obeys."[67]

It's an interesting thought that we can serve God best by being obedient when we least want to, and when we can't even see, hear, feel or detect his presence.

When Jesus tells this parable, he is specifically addressing his disciples. It comes right after another parable, the Householder and the Thief, and continues the theme of the future. Jesus knew the time was approaching when he'd no longer be walking around with his disciples in a bodily way. Jesus needed to prepare them, and teach them how to behave when he was gone.

In this parable a servant was given responsibilities to carry out while the master is away, and the resources to carry them out. The servant was "set over his household", which probably meant a bit more than our typical modern homes, in terms of responsibilities – with maids, cooks, gardeners, farmers… there would have been several servants and a lot of property to steward. A reward is coming to the servant who can follow instructions well, even *while the master is away*. When the master gets back, if he finds that his servant has been obedient, and his household is healthy and well fed, the servant will be blessed

---

[67] I've added the extra words in brackets.

and given great responsibilities, and a position of great honour in the household.

But if the servant acts wickedly, taking advantage of this responsibility while the master is away, then he will get caught out and the punishment will be extreme. He will be cut into pieces and thrown out with the hypocrites, into the place where there is "weeping and gnashing of teeth". For a household servant that would be over the top, but this language is pointing us to the spiritual message; "weeping and gnashing of teeth" is Matthew's term for the eternal torment of *Hell*. Eternal separation from God.

This parable reminds us of something about authority: it is never really ours. All power and authority belongs to God, not to us. Whatever authority we have is *borrowed*, while we act as an agent of God. In that sense *everything* anyone does when in authority is done in God's name... It's no wonder punishments are in store for those who abuse power...

How do we apply this lesson today? The message is specifically addressed *to disciples*, those who say they are believers and followers of Jesus. If we call ourselves Christians (little Christs), we are servants of the Lord, so we can draw a direct line between us and the servant in the parable. Like the servant, *we disciples* have been given responsibilities and instructions to follow.

Like the master of the house, Jesus will return at some unknown point. When he does, we are blessed if we have been obedient. But if we are found partying through God's gifts, neglecting our various duties and/or abusing those we are supposed to be looking after, then the consequences will be dire. The rejection of the bad servant is shocking. When God rejects a false disciple, we can expect it to be fierce.

How did the wicked servant mess it up so badly? It began by doubting the master. "My master is delayed." Meaning, my boss is away, he's taking too long… perhaps he isn't coming back… The beginning of sin doubting God. This is faith slipping away. Like the snake in Eden, the questioning of God is the beginning of the fall. "Did God actually say…?" (Genesis 3:1). As soon as the wicked servant began to doubt the master was returning, look what happened. The *doubt* turned into *disobedience*. The servant started to use the master's resources for himself, partying and drinking his way through them. The servant beat and abused the others. He took the good things he was made a steward of and he used them for his own selfish entertainment.

We know *faith and obedience* are close friends, but *doubt and disobedience* are equally chummy; if you share a meal with one of them, you'll get talking to the other.

So we must be alert to the possibility if we are doubting Jesus will return, we will begin to slip into selfish abuse of what God has entrusted to us. The particular warning here is that Jesus *may come sooner than you expect*, or while you have given up hope.[68] However long the wait is, *faithfulness and obedience* is what is required.

This parable is a warning to continue being obedient even while we don't feel like God is watching us. When Jesus returns – or when our

---

[68] As opposed to the Ten Bridesmaids, which we will consider next, when the bridegroom arrived later than expected.

time is over – we need to be found obeying God, as a faithful servant of his kingdom.

The time will arrive suddenly, and when it does there won't be time to protest. There will be no more forgiveness or second chances.

Questions for reflection:

Having noticed that the master was delayed, what action might a faithful servant have taken?

Is it better to be obedient when we're being watched or in private?

If we keep in mind that everything belongs to God, including all power and authority, how might that help us to obey and prepare for his return?

One thing you can do

Practise dealing with doubt by talking with a Christian friend and asking difficult questions. "Do you feel like God is always watching you?"

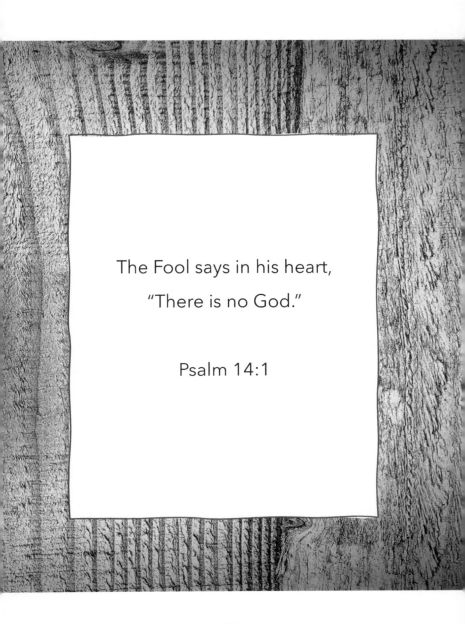

The Fool says in his heart,

"There is no God."

Psalm 14:1

32 Be Prepared to Wait

The Ten Bridesmaids

Matthew 25:1-13

Then the kingdom of heaven will be like ten virgins who took their lamps and went to meet the bridegroom. Five of them were foolish, and five were wise. For when the foolish took their lamps, they took no oil with them, but the wise took flasks of oil with their lamps. As the bridegroom was delayed, they all became drowsy and slept. But at midnight there was a cry, "Here is the bridegroom! Come out to meet him." Then all those virgins rose and trimmed their lamps. And the foolish said to the wise, "Give us some of your oil, for our lamps are going out." But the wise answered, saying, "Since there will not be enough for us and for you, go rather to the dealers and buy for yourselves." And while they were going to buy, the bridegroom came, and those who were ready went in with him to the marriage feast, and the door was shut. Afterwards the other virgins came also, saying, "Lord, lord, open to us." But he answered, "Truly, I say to you, I do not know you." Watch therefore, for you know neither the day nor the hour.

If you're a bit like me, you might empathise with the underprepared, foolish young girls. There's always something I've not thought of. When I go to the beach, other people have chairs. When I go on a picnic, other people have glasses to drink from. When our church decided, for environmental reasons, we should start bringing our own coffee mugs it took me weeks to adapt, and each of those Sundays I was still drinking from the disposable cups of shame. (If I didn't have a more organised wife I probably still would be.) At certain moments, simply being there isn't enough; you need to be *prepared* too…

In the final days of Jesus' ministry, the days between his triumphant arrival in Jerusalem and his arrest and trial, Jesus focussed his teaching on equipping his disciples for the future. We find this in Matthew 24–25. He explained in broad terms what the future will hold, and how they should act in it. The key words are *watchfulness* (the Lesson of the Fig Tree), *wakefulness* (the Householder and the Thief), *obedience* (the Faithful and Unfaithful Servant) and now *preparedness*.

This parable is set at a wedding. Weddings at the time were long celebrations, with events spread over the whole engagement, culminating in a feast where the bride and groom were finally wed. At this event girls carrying lamps would be invited to accompany the bridegroom in, something like bridesmaids today. Then they'd join the wedding feast, where there'd be music, dancing, food and drink. It was the kind of event you could get excited about.[69]

---

[69] Especially in a world without the internet and television.

On this occasion, ten young women got themselves dressed up. They all looked the part. They got themselves to the right place with the right people. They all had their lamps; so far everything was going well. But there was a hidden difference between them that would soon divide the group. Five of them had brought extra oil to refill their lamps; five of them had not.

You'll know how weddings can drag on. Well, the evening got later and later, and the bridegroom still hadn't turned up, so the women became tired. They hadn't given up on the party, so they stayed where they were, but as they waited they gradually drifted off to sleep. They were woken suddenly, by the sound of the bridegroom being announced. They needed to relight their oil lamps... and fast! They trimmed the wicks and fumbled to refill the oil, but... the foolish had none, because only the wise had come prepared for a long night.

But what does it mean to be foolish or wise? We tend to think of foolishness as daftness or silliness. But in the Bible foolishness is about our attitude to God. The fool is the one who says in their heart, "there is no God" (Psalm 14:1). Wisdom, also, is a little different to what we might naturally assume; we might think of wisdom as *figuring everything out for yourself*. But it isn't very wise to trust in your own figuring-out, when divine revelation is available. A *wise person trusts in God*. Wisdom means trusting that if God says he's coming, then he is.

The warning in the previous parable, "The Faithful and Unfaithful Servants", is that the master could arrive sooner than we expect, and catch us out. So we mustn't assume the master is staying away a long time. This parable has a different warning; waiting for the master *might take longer* than we imagine, but at any time a shout could go out, and we need to be ready to move – like the wise young women.

Holding these together, we need to be prepared to live a long and faithful life in the world, *but at the same time* never forget we could be called to Heaven at any moment.

Keeping the two sides in mind, in practice this means every day is a Bible-reading, prayerful, loving-your-neighbour, charitable kind of day – we need to be part of the Kingdom of God today, ready to meet Jesus. But it will also be a going-to-work, teaching-your-children, grocery-shopping, ironing-your-shirts kind of day – because we need to plan for tomorrow as well, in case Jesus doesn't come for us tonight. Every day should (and usually will) be both; it's no good doing one without the other. It's no use getting all dressed up for Jesus to arrive but turning up *without your oil*.

Remember all these women were invited, they all responded and they all were waiting… these women represent the "visible church", meaning the people who at least have the appearance of Christians. But not all of them were prepared for Jesus. When it comes to it you need to have your own "oil". As in the parable, it can't be borrowed from someone else at the last minute. Faith is like this; you cannot rest on the living faith of your church or your family.

Jesus began his story saying the Kingdon of Heaven will be *like this*. The wise girls went into the party with the bridegroom but the unprepared fools missed out. The most chilling part of this story is that failing to prepare can leave you shut out of the Kingdom of Heaven for ever. Even though they came back and knocked on the door, they were still not let in. That's where the parable ended, with the time running out and the door slamming shut. The fools are cut off: "Truly I say to you, I do not know you."

Questions for reflection:

It can be quite abstract to talk about being "prepared" for Jesus to return. What would you be worried about if he knocked on your door right now?

If you knew the timetable for Jesus' return, what would you be doing differently?

One thing you can do

You cannot rely on someone else's "oil" – our faith must be our own – not something we're borrowing from our families or our churches. Take the time today to pray over this parable, talk to God about your *personal* trust in him.

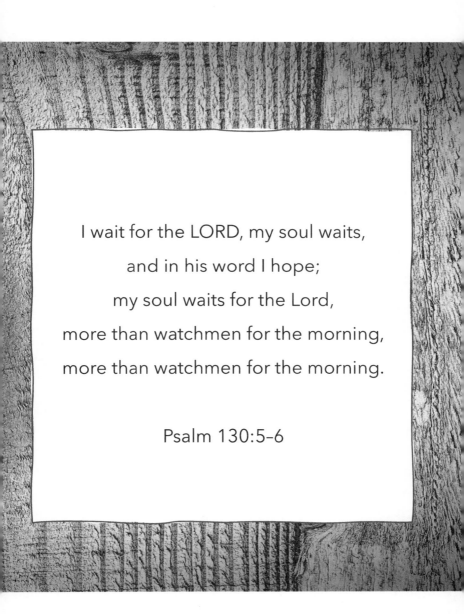

I wait for the LORD, my soul waits,

and in his word I hope;

my soul waits for the Lord,

more than watchmen for the morning,

more than watchmen for the morning.

Psalm 130:5–6

33 Do Something While You Wait

The Talents

Matthew 25:14-30

For it will be like a man going on a journey, who called his servants and entrusted to them his property. To one he gave five talents, to another two, to another one, to each according to his ability. Then he went away. He who had received the five talents went at once and traded with them, and he made five talents more. So also he who had the two talents made two talents more. But he who had received the one talent went and dug in the ground and hid his master's money. Now after a long time the master of those servants came and settled accounts with them. And he who had received the five talents came forward, bringing five talents more, saying, "Master, you delivered to me five talents; here I have made five talents more." His master said to him, "Well done, good and faithful servant. You have been faithful over a little; I will set you over much. Enter into the joy of your master." And he also who had the two talents came forward, saying, "Master, you delivered to me two talents; here I have made two talents more." His master said to him, "Well done, good and faithful servant.

You have been faithful over a little; I will set you over much. Enter into the joy of your master." He also who had received the one talent came forward, saying, "Master, I knew you to be a hard man, reaping where you did not sow, and gathering where you scattered no seed, so I was afraid, and I went and hid your talent in the ground. Here you have what is yours." But his master answered him, "You wicked and slothful servant! You knew that I reap where I have not sown and gather where I scattered no seed? Then you ought to have invested my money with the bankers, and at my coming I should have received what was my own with interest. So take the talent from him and give it to him who has the ten talents. For to everyone who has will more be given, and he will have an abundance. But from the one who has not, even what he has will be taken away. And cast the worthless servant into the outer darkness. In that place there will be weeping and gnashing of teeth."

We're in the last few days before Jesus is killed. Dark clouds[70] are gathering on the horizon. Jesus' thoughts and teaching are fixed on the future, and it's a future his disciples will need to face without him. If history is a road, then it's turning a corner.[71] The final harvest[72] is coming. The disciples will

---

[70] Metaphorical clouds.
[71] A different metaphor.
[72] A third metaphor

have work to do as God's plan for salvation is enacted. Soon Jesus' followers will need to learn obedience *in their master's absence*.

This is the time Jesus tells the "Parable of the Talents", and the plot is like this: three employees are entrusted with quite large sums of money to look after while their boss is away. Without any specific instructions to follow, they have been given a great amount of freedom. They have authority to steward it, and responsibility for the outcome. The money isn't distributed evenly; instead they are given different amounts. The first has been entrusted with the most. The next has about half as much, and the junior has the smallest amount. This reflects the world we live in: we all end up with different resources and different responsibilities.

When he returns he discovers the first two doubled his money and are rewarded. The other one buried it in the ground, and he is punished.

There's a clue to the deeper meaning of the story hiding in the language the master uses. His successful employees are not promoted, or rewarded financially... No, they are commended as "good and faithful servants" and invited to "enter into the master's rest" – not boardroom language but the language of God at the final judgement.

As for the junior employee who displeased the master with his *hide-it-in-the-ground* strategy: is he called for a disciplinary meeting, or given a written warning? Is he fired? No, he's sent to the place where there is "weeping and gnashing of teeth". This is Matthew's language for Hell. Surprising language from your boss – but appropriate language for God.

Jesus was teaching his disciples how to live in the world without him. For three years they have been following their teacher in a literal sense, step by step, and doing whatever they're told. But from now on they will be continuing this work while Jesus is absent, and he wants them to be found working faithfully when judgement time comes.

This parable is about the attitude we need for the day-to-day practical things of the world below; when our hearts belongs to Jesus – in heaven above.

Like the servants in the parable, all of us have been given jobs to do and resources to do them with. Some of us have been given more, some less – but since God is wise and just – we should expect the resources we have been entrusted with will fit the work we are expected to do. And we are supposed to see these resources as the property of our heavenly boss: when he returns, we should expect to be able to show we used them well.

How do we apply this? Firstly, don't duck the warning! We must not twist Jesus' teaching to avoid the message. The temptation, for instance, might be to narrow this parable down to something you don't have very much of – like time – to avoid being generous with something you have more of – like money. Money has a dangerous hold on us, especially (strangely enough) when we have plenty of it. Lots of Christians in the western world are money-rich and time-poor... where it has become common to spiritualise Jesus' teaching on money. But, since a talent is a quantity of money,[73] isn't it a bit stubborn to refuse to apply this lesson to our wealth? So an obvious first application is to treat our money as though it belongs to God – not hoarding it up for ourselves or spending it extravagantly. Our faith should have financial consequences, and our spending habits should be different to the people around us *because of* what we believe. When we have an excess, instead of upgrading our lifestyles we should be on the lookout for people with a need. Both (in fact, *especially*) inside our churches, and outside.

On the other hand, we can broaden it out from money, by adopting the same heart attitude to all other resources, like our time, labour, musical gifts, opportunities, cooking, counselling… we can be faithfully stewarding whatever we have been entrusted with while we wait for the return of our master.

One of the main barriers to faithful stewardship is fear. We fear that if we're generous with our money we won't have enough for ourselves. Or we might fear (for instance) speaking to a friend about Jesus. We risk losing respect, losing an argument, or even losing a friendship – if it goes really badly. You might prefer to play it safe but, if he has entrusted you with an open goal, show some *faith* in his judgement by speaking up and investing this "resource" (which is in this case an opportunity to speak up!). What God has entrusted you with, whether it's money or something else, you are supposed to take hold of and use.

---

[73] Interestingly it is from this parable we get the English term "talent", meaning a gift or ability, which might show how much we want this parable to be about anything except money.

The junior servant showed *fear*. He had a bad impression of his master – he saw the master as a hard and grasping man and was afraid of getting on the wrong side of him. So he played it safe, and did nothing with his master's resource except hide it.

If we see God like the junior servant saw his master – an impossible God we cannot please, a God to be frightened of – we'll also be too frightened to do anything for him.

But, since we have faith in our Lord, who is a wise and fair master, who loves us and is good, is it rational to be afraid to act? Whatever he's given you, whether it's money, time, intelligence, creativity, opportunity or hospitality – whatever it is – we should remember that the Lord has a good purpose for it, and a good purpose for us. During his absence until the time of judgement, he wants us to put his resources to good use. What's more, God is *pleased* when we act like this!

The two servants who traded with their master's money[74] risked losing it – but fear didn't hold them back because they had *faith* in their master. *Trusting* their master's good character, they faithfully set about their work – even though he wasn't guiding their every step. If we have faith in God's good character, we can be better stewards of his resources.

Ask these questions: why have I been given this? What is it for? How can I bless someone with it? How can I grow the Kingdom on earth

---

[74] Burying money in the ground might also feel like a risk but back then it was common practice for security: better than leaving it in a home, and safer than trading it, or probably safer than the banker even.

with it? It is my prayer that everyone reading this will one day hear Jesus say, "Well done, good and faithful servant. You have been faithful over a little; I will set you over much. Enter into the *joy* of your master."

Questions for reflection:

Everything we have is a gift from God. Do you agree?

How do we work out which gifts to enjoy, and which to share or give away for the Kingdom? Is there a difference...?

Think about all the resources you have been given responsibility for. What do you have more of, or less of?

Is there anything you would honestly prefer Jesus not to be talking about? Why?

One thing you can do

Pick up a few of your bank statements and spend a little time going through them. Do a little audit pretending they are someone else's... Can you find evidence they (you!) are a faithful servant?

Some Conclusions

So this is it: we've covered thirty-three of Jesus' parables. Much more could be said about each of them... and even then there are still more parables we could pick out and discuss. But what conclusions can we draw by looking back over them all?

The parables teach us that *how we respond* to the Word of God is important (Two Builders, The Sower). Those of us who *receive* the Word must make it our *whole supporting foundation* and be a *light* to the world (Lamp on a Stand). The Kingdom itself is a *certainty*, starting small but ever *gowing*, through *mysterious* means (Mustard Seed, Seed Growing Secretly). The Kingdom is worth giving *everything* you have to gain entrance (Hidden Treasure, The Pearl). Its citizens are *granted forgiveness* for which they are grateful (Two Debtors) and in turn act with *forgiveness towards others* (Unforgiving Servant). They must *shun worldly obessions* like money (Rich Fool), *love their neighbours* (Good Samaritan) and *pray consistently* and *confidently* (Unjust Judge, Friend at Midnight), trusting that *Jesus has the strength* and power to ultimately deliver them from evil (Strong Man). Until the great *sorting* comes at the end of time (Net, Wheat and the Tares), which could happen *at any moment* (Faithful and Unfaithful Servants, Ten Bridemaids, Householder and Thief, Lesson of the Fig Tree), members of the Kingdom work as *dedicated* (Talents, Unjust Steward) *servants* in the vineyard (Unworthy Servant) and *seeking out the lost* (Lost Sheep and Lost Coin) before *receiving their fair reward*. (Labourers in the Vineyard). But not everyone who expects to be a part of it will inherit their place in the new kingdom (Two Sons, Barren Fig Tree, Wicked

Tenants) and many will reject the offer by *trusting in their own righteousness*. (Pharisee and the Tax Collector).

Which brings us to the greatest challenge of the parables. There is no floating about with Jesus. You can't read his teaching without putting yourself on one side of the fence or the other. Since the parables are full of teaching about the Kingdom; if you don't accept Jesus is *the* king, then there is nothing else to do except reject him entirely, along with all his teaching.

But if you accept Jesus, then these explosive stories are full of valuable instruction about Kingdom living, delivered directly into our hearts from the mouth of your king. Those who listen to them and *consider them carefully* will be learning from the creator of life, the universe and everything.

As Simon Peter said; "Lord, to whom shall we go? You have the words of eternal life, and we have believed, and have come to know, that you are the Holy One of God."

So where do you stand?

Further Reading

While researching this book I read several great resources on the parables. Here are the ones I found most useful, in case you would like to read further:

Interpreting the Parables – Craig L. Blomberg: I especially appreciated his history of parable interpretation detailing all the different approaches (and errors!) over church history.

The Challenge of Jesus' Parables – edited by Richard N. Longenecker: A set of thirteen essays on the subject of the parables.

Parables – John MacArthur: I particularly enjoyed the Good Samaritan.

The Parables of Jesus – Joachim Jeremias: One of the most influential books (of the twentieth century) on the parables.

Stories with Intent – Klyne Snodgrass: A massive resource, an excellent reference for anyone preaching or teaching on the parables.

Others:

Screwtape letters – CS Lewis: As quoted in chapter 31.

The Great Divorce – CS Lewis: Well-known fiction on Heaven and Hell, with plenty to meditate on. Lewis has the credit for the title of Chapter 25.

About the Author

Peter lives with his wife, Francine, and their three children in rural Warwickshire, England. He is a lifelong student of the Bible with a passion for making Jesus' teachings clear, engaging, and relevant for today's world.

Peter is a part of the staff team at St David's Church, Moreton-in-Marsh, where, amongst other things, he takes care of the Bible study small groups, leads courses for faith seekers, prepares families for baptism and is a regular member of the preaching team. Before entering into ministry he trained and worked as an aerospace engineer and ran a business together with Francine.

They are currently considering getting a dog.